Teaching Isn't For Cowards

Only the Strong Survive

Rheba Washington-Lindsey, PhD

iUniverse, Inc.
New York   Bloomington

Teaching Isn't For Cowards
Only the Strong Survive

iUniverse books may be ordered through booksellers or by contacting:

iUniverse
1663 Liberty Drive
Bloomington, IN 47403
www.iuniverse.com
1-800-Authors (1-800-288-4677)

ISBN: 978-1-4502-1883-2 (sc)
ISBN: 978-1-4502-1884-9 (ebook)

Printed in the United States of America

iUniverse rev. date: 06/09/2010

I would like to acknowledge the publishers and/or individuals for permission to reprint the material found in the following stories: *Stepping Into the Lion's Den* and *Monday, Monday and The CartoonStock6*

Dedication

To all who have made the decision to enter the education profession, the decision to touch the lives of students by educating them, encouraging them, and providing them with the tools they will need to become productive citizens: knowledge, discipline, self-respect, heightened thinking, and belief in oneself.

To my dad, my hero, my cheerleader, who wanted my writing to touch the lives of other people. It was he who inspired me to dream of writing and who envisioned me soaring high, like an eagle. It was my dad who envisioned me as a teacher. It was Dad who said in his strong, stern voice, "Rheba, I believe the Lord is calling you to teach." And, I responded, "Dad, I'm not going to teach. There are too many teachers in this family." Dad replied, "You are to write, speak, teach, and lead. There are kids whose lives can be touched by you."

I thank God for the opportunity to share my experiences, skills, and expertise. Without His guidance this book would have gone with me into the other side.

This book is dedicated to teachers who are courageous, compassionate, dedicated, and focused and whose desire is to be exemplary teachers

I dedicate this book to my husband, Roy Lindsey, who offered me so much of his patience and support and gave thirty years of hard work as a teacher. Finally, I dedicate this book to my daughter, Leah, who wanted to see her grandpa's dream come to pass and who believed that my stories would enrich the lives of other teachers.

Contents

Introduction

Teaching is a humble calling. I have been a member of the teaching profession for thirty years and have attained Highly Qualified Teacher credentials, administrator's credentials, and a master's degree in education. With my experience and the extensive research that has come with it, I know that not all of those who think they have the calling are prepared to teach; some in the classroom may be just barely surviving. About thirteen years ago, I began to take a closer look at teaching. In order to better understand the phenomena of teaching; teachers, students, pedagogy, and working collaboratively with parents and administrators, I found it essential for me to remove myself from the nature of the classroom. I needed to understand why teachers were leaving the profession, why teachers seemed not to be able to handle their classes, why some teachers were popular or well liked by students and others weren't. The steps I took thirteen years ago ultimately resulted in this book. I used my psychology background and mentored and observed teachers as a means of bringing meaning to teaching and the teacher, and of understanding why teachers, including me, are so disgruntled with the teaching profession. Teaching is an art that has changed over the years. That art has changed because our students have changed. To understand these changes, I researched how communicating across cultural lines impacts learning. My research resulted in another master's degree, a book, and the understanding that "culture matters." Those of you who have been in the profession thirty years or more can attest to the fact that the biggest problem you might have had was with "gum chewing in class." Today, gum chewing is minor. Similarly, there was a time when teachers remained in the profession thirty years or longer. Now, according to statistics gathered by the National Education Association, the average new teacher remains in the classroom less than five years. There was a time when school districts carefully and meticulously searched for the best teachers; teaching was competitive. Now, school districts anxiously attempt to fill classroom openings with warm bodies. They are so desperate for teachers that they hire people who have degrees in any subject matter, who use teaching as an expression to "give back" and are willing to get teaching credentials without student teaching. Unfortunately, the teacher and administrator don't take into account that teaching isn't for everybody. It may not have been the best profession for the following teacher:

"I've just completed my fifth week of school. I certainly didn't expect what I encountered. My smallest social studies class has thirty-two students in it. I had trouble getting students to do the assignments; I had trouble writing the district's standards into the lesson plans; and I feel overwhelmed with paperwork." She continued, "The school vice-principal, my supervisor, and the counselor promised that my social studies classes would be level by October if not before. The vice-principal stated, 'Our kids have some social problems but they are not real bad.' Well, maybe our definition of 'bad' is different. Most of my classes have students who are above bad. They entered the class noisily, hassled one another with foul mouths—even the girls used obscene words. They sat on top of the desk and ignored my requests to sit down and do the lesson—a lesson that took me hours to prepare. All I can say is, 'What am I doing here? This is not teaching. These students are not interested in learning.'"

Teaching other people's children is like opening a surprise package; you will find challenges, stress, fulfillment, tears, laughter, excitement, and inspiration. There is a strong driving force that is keeping teachers from surviving in the classroom.

Teaching Isn't For Cowards is a collection of personal teaching memoirs gathered from my experience as a teacher and administrator in Brownwood State Home and School, Brownwood, Texas; Clark County School District, Las Vegas, Nevada; Franklin McKinley School District, San Jose, California. I share the joys, ills, surprises, and rewards I have encountered as a teacher. I have met teachers whose hearts are in teaching but who find teaching becoming more difficult because of the swelling numbers of such concerns as poor academic achievers, student apathy, overcrowded classrooms, and unruly student behavior. Many teachers have also experienced increasing instructional demands and, more important, scrutiny; a lack of parent and community support; and a lack of administrative support. Classroom teachers find themselves agitated, dismayed, and besieged by a profession that is meant to serve and prepare students to become productive citizens.

Research confirms that teaching is filled with positive, self-fulfilling attributes. Yet there looms a downside of teaching that takes its toll on teacher morale. This book reveals what the research says about the hidden dark side of teaching that student teaching failed to convey. You'll be able to learn new research-based principles of teaching and apply those principles in your classroom. For example, you'll understand why students are labeled "reluctant learners," and what teachers can do to adapt their instruction so that even the "unmotivated learner" wants to learn.

You'll be able to identify your management style and analyze and compare it with the ideal management style, and develop strategies for improving your classroom management. You'll understand why teaching should be reserved for individuals who aren't afraid to use tough love in the classroom. I've been in one classroom where the students were actually throwing books at the teacher; in another class, a student threw gum at the teacher and it landed in her hair. If you are in a place where discipline, which is different from management, is running you instead of you running it, you'll be given useful discipline tools that you can use in the classroom. For example, how would you respond to a student who is consistently rude to you, interrupts your instruction, and disrupts the learning environment? What would you do with a student who "got in your face" during a lesson?

B.F. Skinner's model of positive reinforcement still works. Students, like teachers, want pats on the back for a job well done or, even better, something tangible. Skinner taught us that human beings perform better when they get something for their efforts. But some psychologists warn that giving too many tangible gifts may not be good for our students. Find out what the research says about rewarding students for academic achievement.

Teaching Isn't for Cowards is like a health book. You'll find this book to be unique in that it provides an easy-to-follow recipe for facing the issues in teaching. It is a wake-up call for those interested in entering the education profession. Unlike in many memoirs, my stories are augmented with research. *Teaching Isn't for Cowards* is not only about facing students today, but also about looking at the education profession with optimism for the future.

I hope you find the book uplifting and gain insight and encouragement from it. And I hope you enjoy reading it as much as I enjoyed writing it. Here's to teaching!

1. HERE I AM, SEND ME

"Don't be afraid to take a big step if one is indicated. You can't cross a chasm in two small jumps."

— *David Lloyd George*

"I give the same advice to all new teachers.
Pretend you know what you are doing."

Practically Indispensable

"The credit belongs to the man who is actually in the arena; whose face is marred by dust and sweat and blood; who strives valiantly; who errs and comes short again and again; who knows the greatest enthusiasms, the great devotions, and spends himself in a worthy cause/who at the best knows in the end that triumph of high achievement; and who at the worst, if he fails, at least fails daring greatly."

— *Theodore Roosevelt*

Even though in principle we are all dispensable and can be replaced, replacing someone who has had a significant impact in an organization is not always easy. The same holds true with teachers. Finally, indispensable teachers are like precious jewels; they exude dynamism that clearly influences learning. Does a supervisor's evaluation really indicate whether or not a teacher is indispensable? Don't count on it. I shivered as I wondered if my classroom epitomized a caring classroom and wondered if my students would portray me as an indispensable teacher. We all know that there is a short supply of really dedicated, good educators. As many people employed in the private sector lose their jobs and suffer from cutbacks, more of them are seriously thinking of going into the teaching profession. But, will they be indispensable teachers? People who move into the teaching market, for whatever reason, may not be prepared or have the required skills necessary to classroom management. They may not know how to engage students in a learning activity to ensure that they are learning or even to construct an assessment that measures learning. Educators who are indispensable have special qualities, such as the ability to influence, inspire, and affect change in others. Indispensable teachers feel deeply about their students; they may even see themselves as surrogate parents. There are some factors that distinguish indispensable teachers from average teachers.

First, indispensable teachers emanate from within: they are willing to give of themselves and their time; they expend energy in order to advance the mission of the "company." These individual look for the good in others and do not boast of themselves. Teachers need to know how to bond with their students; in other words, they must be able to build relationships. This is a quality that certainly puts success on the map. Knowing their students allows teachers to determine what level of expectations to have for those students.

According to Pendergast and Bahr (2006), building positive student-teacher relationships is incumbent upon being respectful and supportive. Motshinig-Pitrik and White (2004) take relationship building to another level by defining it as a relationship built upon being empathetic, real, and amicable. I have found that when I take time to develop a positive relationship with students I usually see some improvement in their academic and behavior performance. It's as though students felt that I was watching them, when in fact, I might have been without realizing that they were experiencing a measure of improvement. Research by Pianta (1999) supports my allegations. He confirms that when there is a close relationship with teachers there is a higher level of student achievement. Stipek (2006) suggest that students put forth more effort toward achieving academic success and behavior improvement when teachers treat them humanly while taking a sincere interest in them in school as well as outside of school. The end result is active motivation, self-initiative, positive engagement, and ultimately success. This reminds me a time when I desperately needed to build a relationship with students in my remedial reading class, students who are underachievers. I had one student in my second period class, Patrick, who just couldn't get with the reading program. Patrick was a quiet guy, didn't bother to socialize with other students, and had an extremely unorganized notebook. In fact, many days I had to loan him a pencil and a sheet of paper. He was polite with "Yes ma'am and no ma'am." I would guide him into an assignment, return after ten minutes to check on him, and he wouldn't have moved from where I led him. His mind drifted and he was easily distracted. One day I decided to get to know Patrick better. I began with small talk: "What did you do over the weekend?" "Are you the only child?" "What's your favorite sport or thing to do?" Slowly, day-by-day I got to know Patrick. I finally got up the nerve to challenge Patrick to clean out his notebook over the weekend. That Monday his notebook was cleaned out. As a reward and a need, I gave him a pen/pencil holder in which to place his writing instruments. Shortly thereafter this young man became the most motivated, engaged, focused student I had. His grade went from an "F" to an "A." Spending a little time to build a relationship paid big dividends.

Being a good employee is not rare, but being an outstanding employee is extraordinary and rare, just like a precious African gem. I once read a story (West, 1990) about an employee who worked for an electric company. The employee could be depended on to go out anywhere in the city, in any kind of weather—cold, rainy, snowy, stormy; no matter how dangerous it was, he would get the job done. He never complained or turned down his boss's request for help. After finishing a job, he would always say with pride, "I just love to see the lights come on." Indispensable teachers echo the words of the employee above. "I just love to hear the voices of children coming down the hall," they might say, or, "I just can't wait to see my students." There were plenty of times when I was disgruntled and began to complain, protesting, "There are just too many demands on us," or, "The students are poor performers in spite of the extra time I have spent helping them to do better." The list of complaints is long: The students are apathetic, the administration is not supportive, there is a lack of parent support, and there is little opportunity for creativity. Despite all of these concerns, indispensable teachers remain motivated, enthusiastic, professional, responsible, and achievement oriented.

Second, indispensable teachers have determination, like the lion in *The Wizard of Oz*. Their determination is carried over into their work performance, as they excel and work hard at being the best teachers and experts in their fields. For example, my high school department chair made the following announcement at the beginning of the year: "Lindsey, you do well with failing students. You seem to relate to those types of students; I don't. So, I've assigned you three Remedial English classes and two Basic English classes and could really use your help with teaching after-school English for juniors and seniors who have yet to pass the English portion of the proficiency test." You're teaching in a high school with a high dropout rate, increasing student behavior problems, teen pregnancies, low student morale, lack of parent participation. Students from low socioeconomic status require an abbreviated curriculum—something very different from the traditional curriculum, materials, and instruction. You have at-risk students who are in danger of failing. Trying to get them motivated about their education is challenging, often disheartening, and frustrating. You seldom see immediate academic results. How would an indispensable teacher respond to this scenario? Indispensable teachers must be prepared to encounter unanticipated errors or problems in their lesson plans, goals, or learning activities. Teaching a large number of potential students who had not passed the proficiency test would mean anticipating errors and misconceptions, and allowing for misplanning. However, I was charged with helping students move toward passing the test and developing a deeper understanding of three skill areas: reading, writing, and test taking.

Indispensable teachers willingly accept any assignments placed before them. One year, the department chair assigned me all of the basic classes. These classes consisted of students who had extremely low reading skills (3.0–4.5), third-fourth grade of the fifth month, students who could not write a complete sentence; this meant they were not proficient in English. I accepted the assignment, but it was not all joy. No matter. I was unwilling to give anything less than A+ effort. Was it challenging? You betcha! Was it frustrating? You betcha! Did I have to go out on a limb? You betcha! Was it a blessing in the end? You betcha!

Third, an indispensable person challenges the assumption(s) of others in order to demonstrate greatness, knowledge of pedagogical coursework, and credibility to the organization or profession (Bishay, 1996). Teachers should be highly capable of identifying the learning styles of students, identifying students' motivational levels, and developing learning strategies that will increase and attract students to the learning process. The story of Ashiti is a good example. Ashiti was the only Native American student enrolled out of some 168 students in my English class. He didn't hesitate to let me know that getting an education was not his top priority, and it showed: Ashiti had a serious attendance problem. He slept in class and seldom, if ever, participated in any class lessons. Reaching Ashiti was challenging. I wanted to show him that I was concerned. Maybe he could do a special group project; this would give him an opportunity to interact with a small number of his classmates. I decided to speak with him about his excessive absences.

Maybe there was a good reason or something the school could do to get him interested in school and thus improve his attendance.

I began searching for ways to include him in the educational curriculum; that meant I had to take additional professional development classes and learn about his tribal customs, values, and beliefs. It is this willingness to do whatever it takes to motivate a student that makes teachers indispensible.

The fourth characteristic of indispensable teachers is that they are achievement-oriented (Bishay, 1996). The trick was to get Ashiti to believe there would be personal gain for him. I urged him to ask himself a couple of questions. The first was, "What's in it for me?" I hoped he would not respond with, "Nothing. I'm a loser anyway." If he had, I would have been fighting a losing battle. Maybe if he asked himself, "Will getting an education advance my culture?" he would see the light. I set out to motivate Ashiti to be a successful student in his English class and to envision the long-term value for himself and his culture. I was able to get someone to check on the issue of his attendance. I transformed the entire classroom environment in several ways, three of which helped to make the learning environment multiethnic-friendly: I put up posters of different ethnic groups and success stories from their communities, including the Sioux tribe; I rethought my instructional method, making it simple, functional, and pleasurable; and I put extra effort into making the lessons failure-free. I used student groups (small, not more than three); I placed students with partners and in cohorts of five students to encourage student learning and participation. This helped to bring Ashiti out of his shyness, fear of failure, and negative attitude. The indispensable teacher is the one who lives every class as if it were something new, adding excitement that will change a student's life.

Fifth, good teachers know how to discipline undisciplined students with no fear. I once taught next to a young fellow who decided that he wanted to leave his chosen profession and become a teacher. He was extremely smart, a great writer, and highly successful in the business he was leaving. He had successfully completed some teacher education programs. But he had a hard time adjusting to the classroom situation; he soon found out that the classroom experience was not like his office experience. Every class period, I found myself in his room settling his students, disciplining where necessary so that he could teach an English lesson. He simply didn't understand what teaching was all about. He didn't understand the student culture or how to discipline, and when he did discipline, he was shy about it. He had no clue as to how to write lesson plans and certainly lacked knowledge about engaging in learning activities. He ended up resigning at the end of the year. The students had kicked him out. Teaching isn't for everybody.

A sixth distinguishing characteristic of indispensable teachers is their knowledge of managing the classrooms. Teachers need to know that "management" is effectively applying provisions and procedures necessary for establishing and maintaining decorum that embraces a learning environment (Duke, 1979). How a teacher manages his or her classroom speaks to the teacher's understanding of the content—and the learning process.

Many of you are indispensable. This is the time to evaluate yourself. The questionnaire below can be used to assess where you stand. Don't wait for your supervisor to determine if you are indispensable. You do that. Using a five-point scale—5=Strongly agree, 4=Agree very much, 3=Agree somewhat, 2=Agree, and 1=Disagree—determine if you are indispensable by answering the following questions: Do I work well with coworkers? Do I seize opportunities to grow professionally? Do I look forward to challenging the minds of my students with new ideas? Am I bored with my job? Does the curriculum allow me to utilize my skills and other talents in the learning process? Does my administrator provide me with additional training or professional development? Does my administrator offer me opportunities for periodic changes from the classroom environment? Does my school district offer opportunities for changes from the classroom environment? Do I find my work challenging? Does my school district allow me to become involved in the decision-making structures? Do I have a sense of empowerment in my school? Does my administrator recognize my accomplishments? Am I a valued teacher in my school? Does my administrator let me know that she/he values my presence and the work I do with other people's children? Am I excited about going to work?

Indispensable teachers are respectful. They practice confidentiality, show sensitivity to feelings, and refrain from making embarrassing comments. Indispensable teachers show compassion to their students. They realize that students make cruel, hurtful comments and maliciously act out at times. An indispensable teacher steps in and offers resolution.

For example, make certain all students are included in student activities, encourage students to practice acts of kindness, and discourage students from engaging in bullying activities. Indispensable teachers develop a sense of belonging in their students' classrooms.

To add to and summarize the characteristics I've mentioned, indispensable teachers are prepared, know their students, have a sense of humor, and are excellent classroom managers and great disciplinarians. They establish high expectations and are trustworthy and loyal to their colleagues.

I will suggest that there is a direct correlation between the characteristics of indispensable teachers and academic performance in their students. We all want our students to have positive school experiences, and putting the indispensable characteristics in place will encourage, motivate, and ultimately result in a successful year for teachers and, hopefully, all students.

You Are Unique:
Qualities of a Good Teacher

Men never moan over the opportunities lost to do well, only the opportunities to be bad.

—*Greek Proverb*

You may equate "work" with "job." They are not the same. Let me explain. According to Mary Welchel, "Our job is what we do day-in and day-out to bring in income. It is the duties we perform. Our work," she continues, "is what God has designed for us to do. It is our purpose for being here, what we are uniquely created for." Therefore, you should be using all of your personal gifts in your line of work. Teachers are chosen based on their special or unique qualities for a particular line of work. These unique qualities often define how successful teachers are at doing their life's work.

We strive so hard to be successful teachers. But you are already a success, simply because you have committed yourself to teaching other people's children. You've probably seen the sign that reads "Only serious applicants need apply." When you signed your contract, you made an oath: "I am committed to teaching other people's children, regardless of race, creed, or economic background." Perhaps the thought of job opportunities crossed your mind. You may recall getting a card from your students and perhaps one of the phrases used was "you are unique," or "to a very special teacher." As an elementary teacher, I received endless cards with these words. Those cards really made me feel important. Teaching elementary school was extremely rewarding for me. My students always showered me with gifts; they were eager learners and their parents were extremely supportive. When you put teachers with special qualities in the classroom, things happen. I'm thinking of such qualities as being positive, even in a bad situation, dependable or reliable, compassionate, flexible, knowledgeable, patient, creative and extremely organized, focused, committed, and enthusiastic. Let's talk further about these qualities.

Many times we meet needs in our personal lives by running from one profession to another carrying around a tub with hurts, disappointments, and discouragements and hoping that teaching will fill that void. It's the person who suddenly feels as though he or she wants to give back to the community, or the teacher who wasn't making it in the corporate world and decided to become a teacher. Teaching will not always fill a void or cure an emotional problem. Many go into the teaching profession to fill an emotional need, but you may not be a match or called to teach. It may make your life worse. This is not a scare tactic. For those of you who are not certain that you have been called to teaching or heard that small voice, you can rest assured that you can be a useful vessel for touching the lives of students. But if you are coming from another profession or you are not certain of the calling, I want to share my personal thoughts and I do hope that they will be a starting point for you. Teaching is not only an opportunity to extend knowledge to other people's kids, but it means you must: know how to manage the classroom, know the subject matter, know how to teach the subject matter, know how to diversify instruction, have strong interpersonal skills, know how to create a caring and challenging learning environment, be able to use interdisciplinary, integrated instruction, and know how to acquire knowledge of your students as individuals and use that knowledge to help develop students' literacy. That's quite a big list.

There have been numerous research studies conducted on the qualities of great teachers. All of the qualities reported were not alike; however, there were many similarities. Allow me to share some of the characteristics of great teachers. First, a great teacher is knowledgeable of students and the subject matter he or she is undertaking. These are the same teachers who know how to engage students in activities that will lead to academic achievement. These are teachers who are knowledgeable about expectations and understand the importance of establishing high expectations. Establishing strong or high expectations for students is imperative.

Teaching is not about what you feel but about what you know you can do and how you can effect change in kids. For example, "I feel that I know the needs of students." It may mean spending extra hours beyond the school hours honing your skills, since spending extra preparation time is closely connected to knowing the subject area. Honing your subject may mean you will need to find a mentor or go out of your way to learn more about what you teach or take professional development classes. You become the "expert" in your subject area and you are expected to live up to that role.

A second unique quality of teachers is their "courage and determination," like the lion in *The Wizard of Oz*. I suppose it's very much like being a positive thinker. A teacher is the person who looks inside a behavior problem or a student who is experiencing poor academic performance. The determination quality is found when the teacher does something positive about a negative situation, uses strategies to remove obstacles, or takes steps to encourage a problem student. Little did I know that establishing high expectations would cause me to be the target of controversy with many building principals.

Third, great teachers demonstrate how committed they are to their students, the school, and the district's goals. These are teachers who have assessed student learning using their district's guidelines and, along with their school staffs, have a sense of community commitment and collective responsibility in addressing the school improvement plan. Great teachers select appropriate materials to ensure that students have an opportunity to succeed. They also provide variety and creativity in their lessons.

A fourth attribute of great teachers is their ability to communicate and collaborate with other teachers within and across disciplines, specialists, the administration, and parents in order to meet state standards and assessments and create consistency in the school's and district's programs.

If you answer no or none to any of the following questions, you are confessing to not using opportunities to be a unique, great educator:

Am I enthusiastic every morning about coming to work?

Would I be willing to recruit other teachers to work in my school district?

Have I used my teaching, leadership, or mentoring skills within my building in the last six months?

Have I taken the initiative to do something without being told that would showcase my school?

Have I attended any college classes or professional development classes that would enhance my skills so I can better serve my school district?

Have I volunteered to conduct a teacher in-service at my school or in my school district?

Good teachers are enthusiastic about teaching and learning, and that is communicated to their students. These are the teachers who can't wait for the next working day, who stay beyond their contract hours, who take papers home, who get students motivated and stimulate thinking, who communicate with parents, who care about their students' success. But, what happens when a teacher's enthusiasm hits a low? According to the article *Teacher Morale* (ERIC Digest, 1998), low teacher morale has taken the wind out of teachers. Many teachers are no longer as enthusiastic about teaching as they once were. I can remember the last five years of my teaching as being the most hectic time of my career; I had three preps, an increased class size, a curriculum binder that was constantly being added to, and an increase in disruptive students accompanied by a decrease in parent support or interest. There were times when my enthusiasm went out the door. I was stretched to the limit, a major problem facing many teachers. Teacher morale is closely related to enthusiasm, as they both begin with one's thoughts, feelings, state of mind, and mental and emotional attitude. Interestingly, Stenlund (1995) reports that "teachers' perceptions of students and student learning can also affect their morale or enthusiasm." Stenlund's cross-cultural study revealed that teachers' enthusiasm or discouragement is largely predicated on their perceptions of the students and the learning environment. Not surprisingly, teachers look to students' responsiveness and their enthusiasm as important factors that may dictate their own enthusiasm.

A sixth distinguishing quality of good teachers is their ability to manage their classrooms. According to research conducted on classroom management (Duke, 1979), classroom management is not, as it was previously understood, creating a learning environment that is orderly, nor is it reducing misbehaviors. Rather, it is defining strategies that create learning environments; it is increasing and identifying appropriate behaviors that, when used, will yield academic achievement. Thus, what determines "the strength and durability of the primary program, or vector of action," (Evertson, 2006) is the quality of classroom management: time management procedures such as appropriate pacing and well-planned instruction-to-activity transition. Further, there is the element of teaching functions—attention to prerequisites, guided practice, and systematic reviews.

Finally, good teachers know how to discipline undisciplined students and are not afraid to discipline. I recently read about research that used a different paradigm for researching discipline. Hicks and McNary (2004) conducted research on teacher discipline procedures by interviewing students. The purpose of their research was to examine the students' perspectives on teacher behavior that impeded or contributed to effective classroom discipline. They interviewed 182 students (one hundred males and eighty-two females) in fourteen different schools. Their results identified six ingredients that teachers failed to adhere to in their classrooms: teachers did not identify standards for behavior early in the school year, they did not enforce the rules of conduct, they often threatened students who misbehaved but failed to apply consequences for misbehaviors or rule violation. Teachers lacked confidence, were afraid of students or were too strict, leaving no room for humor. Students involved in the research further note that effective disciplinarians were willing to establish positive, caring student-teacher relationships. Teachers need to understand that effective discipline, content knowledge, and instructional strategies make up one's teaching style. What you do in the classroom is reflected in student achievement.

The Awakening

Occasionally in life there are moments of unutterable fulfillment, which cannot be completely explained by those symbols called words. The inaudible language of the heart can only articulate their meanings.

— *Martin Luther King, Jr.*

You've landed your first contract, teaching high school. You're excited, expecting to change the world of education; nothing can stop you. But there is an awakening that comes with being a young teacher in a high school classroom. The first day of school arrives, and suddenly you discover that all of your students are physically larger, and taller than you, in a class of thirty-five or more; that can be scary, and intimidating on one hand, but lead to some defining lessons on the other. That can be scary, intimidating, and it can open doors to serious discipline problems. Next, you're plagued with questions: What do I do if a student curses me out? If I ask my students why they didn't do homework, will they respond with arrogance? What do I say when one of my girls asks me to go to the bathroom? Finally, what should I do if a student becomes angry with me? These are legitimate concerns that all new teachers need to deal with before heading into that high school classroom (Gaut, 2002). There are tactics you can use.

There is certainly something special about venturing into new horizons—the bustling environment, unfamiliar faces, and unforeseen challenges. There is always something joyful about changing schools; there is hope that a new situation will bring something better.

Sometimes moving on releases one from insurmountable expectations, overwhelming performance demands, and the tyranny of teaching the same type of students. Moving on is like a breath of fresh air; it is a simple respite to a tired, bored soul that causes the soul to "shout" for joy. It was during my sixth year of teaching that I decided to move to high school. I was ready for something new. There would be no more routine experiences, only extraordinary and unfamiliar adventures. Those adventures ended up being heightened challenges.

The high school I transferred to was an older high school that attracted 70 percent African-American students, 15 percent Hispanic students, and 15 percent other. It was located in North Las Vegas, Nevada. It had the highest dropout rate, highest crime rate, and highest absentee rate in the school district. This was a school where I would spend much of my teaching career with students I would take special interest in and teachers who would become lifelong acquaintances. It was a place where I would experience tremendous professional and personal growth.

The first day of school was traumatic. The hallways were as noisy as a football stadium; I watched uneasily as my students entered the class; I hoped they did not see the sweat dripping from my forehead or notice my cracking voice as I greeted them, as a means of building a positive relationship with my students. I'd often been greeted with, "Good morning, Mrs. Lindsey." But today, it was, "Whassup?" *Wow!* *They are like giants compared to me,* I remember thinking They towered over me. I was impressed by the way most of the students dressed. This was certainly a change from elementary and middle school.

Before we could begin the instruction and learning process, I knew that establishing classroom rules would be necessary, something I wanted to avoid. Anyway, policies were established with me coming up with most of them. Looking back, I wish I had allowed this to be more student-directed. I enthusiastically began developing, organizing, and teaching reading with a sense of confidence. I knew that it also would be both exhilarating and challenging, but I was up for the challenge. The program was soon off and running. I had invested a lot of time into developing the reading lessons and decorating the room. I worked feverishly to ensure that every inch of the program would be devoted to meeting the diverse reading needs of my students. I greeted each day with renewed spirit—in both mind and body—and new fervor. September passed quickly, but not without some new adventure each day.

My students had a great sense of humor, so we read stories that were interesting and that they could easily relate to. We even read an up-to-date version of *Macbeth*. My students decided they wanted to put on a play for another reading class, so they creatively rewrote *Romeo and Juliet*. They created the setting, props, and even the costumes. I was beyond myself, as the other reading and English classes had not dared such a venture. This earned me a letter of commendation from my administrator. Now, I was really sittin' high, but not too high. I had an appreciation for my students, and let them know it. "I really enjoyed all of you participating in today's activity. I know you'll learn a lot about Shakespeare's work as a result of your reading activities." "Pam, thanks for being such a good leader, and helping your group come up with a creative introduction." And, "Thomas, you guys are on your way to putting together great costumes for the play." I didn't have motivational words for Kevin. Something must be going wrong in his world. The semester moved right along, and I remained exhilarated, until I met my first real challenge with my fourth-period class that would awaken me to the reality of being a teenager.

This was my remedial class, consisting of ten females and eleven males. Not only did my fourth period have remedial reading problems, but also they had exceptional behavior problems—exceptional meaning they were not the kind of behaviors that needed to be constantly refereed. Teachers must have a large tablespoon of patience with their students. The typical misbehavior was excessive talking sprinkled with some spicy vocabulary, nothing drastic. I took measures to ensure that misbehaviors were held at a minimum by keeping my students constantly engaged: warm-up games were played, certificates were given out. I kept my eyes open for what they did right. I struggled with bringing this class up to where my basic students were; I guess I wanted to clone my average group. I felt like the parent who says, "Why can't you be like your brother or sister?" They were capable, yet this class brought a lot of baggage with them. I thought we might tackle some of their issues inside of an adjusted reading curriculum.

One of the three students who did not want to participate in a student writing assignment was Kevin. Okay, here's where a teacher needs a lot of compassion. He had a tattoo on his shoulder and an arrow earring in his right ear. He always wore black—black jeans, black shirt, black shoes, and black faux-leather jacket. Kevin was slender and rather tall; he stood as though he prided himself on his good looks, which certainly did not correlate with his grades. Kevin was usually pretty decent with me compared to the way he interacted with his other teachers. Kevin was arrogant, he did not work, he back-talked, and he was excessively tardy. He would sit in the back of class combing his coal-black, shoulder-length hair. One day, when told, not asked, to put the comb away, Kevin got an attitude. "Why? It's not hurting anybody." He got up, threw the comb in the garbage can, and slowly walked back to his seat. All of this drama interrupted the lesson. Disciplining high school students can be intimidating; I can just see myself disciplining a six-foot, 190-pound guy like Kevin. I never knew if he was a motorcycle wannabe, a Satan worshiper, or worse. One day Kevin entered my class with huge scratches on his face. I approached him carefully while other students worked and asked if he was all right. He said, "I'm a little sleepy, my temper is short, I don't wanna be here, my head hurts, and I definitely am not with the program." His entire demeanor reeked of mutated anger.

My heart ached for Kevin, and understanding him became an important variable. I decided to leave him alone. He was in too much physical and mental pain to bother anybody. It was another two days before Kevin would open up and share the details of his emotional and physical bruises. His mother had jumped him. I responded with, "What an awful situation!" And it did not end there. About three weeks later, Kevin came to school with additional bruises, including a big, swollen black eye and a bleeding fat lip. I found it increasingly difficult to concentrate on teaching, as I watched Kevin wrestle with the heavy weight of not only his bruises, but also the relationship between him and his mother. For a couple of days, Kevin trudged through the daily lessons with such despondency that he became lifeless and listless, and he seemed to care little for life. That seemed like so much pain for a young man to go through.

Kevin privately explained that he and his mother exchanged punches, but this time he refused to allow her to beat him up. As Kevin explained, "She threw the first punch and I hit her back. Wherever she hit me is where I hit her. At one point, she began hitting me with a rolling pin. So I grabbed it and banged her head. Then she ran and grabbed a large pan. I didn't think she would dare hit me, but she did. So I ran to the cupboard while she was kicking me, and managed to get my hands on a frying skillet. Since she hit me with a pan, I fired back with a pan. I hit her upside the head, just like she did me. I soon found myself dodging flying glass; she was throwing glasses, cups, and plates. She didn't hit me. I guess when she got a hold of a butcher knife, it was over. She actually came after me and cornered me; I dared her to stick it in me. All she did was cuss me out and then told me to 'get outta her house.'"

By the time Kevin had finished telling his story, I was terrified. I knew it was up to me to do something. This was child abuse. I alerted Kevin's counselor so that the necessary report of suspected child abuse could be filed, and I requested a parent conference with regard to Kevin's grades. Kevin was a senior and needed to pass the class as well as the proficiency test. I needed his mother's assistance. His mother confirmed Kevin's story. Together we came up with a graduation plan for Kevin, and then Kevin and I came up with some short-term plans for putting the puzzle pieces of his life back together.

Being compassionate is the beginning of living as servants. Teaching inspires us to be compassionate servants to our students. Sometimes the act of being compassionate is the most humbling act a teacher can perform. This became a learning process for me. Kevin's experience opened my eyes to another element of teaching: being sensitive to our students, being compassionate and of genuine service. We have to be careful not to build walls of insensitivity that may hinder the penetration of human wholeness, allowing ourselves to become contemptuous in our teaching; this would make us ineffective in building positive student relationships.

Kevin had to endure pain, suffering, and anguish before he was able to get help. It was not because his teachers thought he was "tough" and he could handle anything that came along. His teachers were not aware of his pain because they were too consumed with getting through the textbook and maintaining classroom order. Everyone needs caring for in some way. Kevin needed it now. Kevin's story brought tears to my eyes, pierced my heart, and made me shudder inwardly. Yes, I wept for Kevin, just as Jesus wept. I weep for other students like Kevin who sit in classrooms, suffering unseen and alone, who have yet to become vulnerable to the point of sharing their story. T.S. Eliot, in his poem *Little Gidding*, further defines my thoughts:

If you came this way,

Taking the route you would be likely to take
From the place you would be likely to come from,
If you came this way in May time, you would find the hedges
White again, in May, with voluptuary sweetness.
It would be the same at the end of the journey,
If you came at night like a broken king,
If you came be day not knowing what you came for,
It would be the same, when you leave the rough road
And turn behind the pigsty to the dull façade
And the tombstone. And what you thought you came for
Is only a shell, a husk of meaning
From which purpose breaks only when it is fulfilled
If at all. Either you had no purpose
Or the purpose is beyond the end you figured
And is altered in fulfillment. There are other places
Which also are the world's end, some at the sea jaws,
Or over a dark lake, in a desert or a city—
But this is the nearest, in place and time.

2. THE ROAD AHEAD OF ME

"The will to do springs from the knowledge that we can do."

—*James Allen*

"I look forward to my first year as a teacher. I wrote lesson plans, attended in-service workshops, and decorated my classroom. Preparation is half the victory. It's the other half that concerns me."

Stepping into the Lion's Den

No one should teach who is not in love with teaching.

— *Margaret E. Sangster*

Blast, here they come! Teaching at a school where students are out of control is never a welcome or wholesome sight. But what would happen if the school environment were conducive to academic success, instead of having graffiti on the walls or wads of paper carelessly thrown on the floor or holes bashed into the walls? What would it be like to teach at a school where students showed their respect for staff and administrators in a general student assembly instead of booing? What would it be like if students showed how extensive their vocabularies were, instead of using expletives and not knowing how to spell them? What would it be like if students were held responsible for their misbehavior? Finally, what would it be like if students and their parents were held responsible for poor academic performance?

Teaching is a very honorable profession, but it is not easy. A good teacher must know the subject matter, have acceptable classroom management skills, and know how to tame the lions in a den. He or she must know what to say and not to say to an administrator, be able to provide interesting instruction, and have strategies for involving parents in the educational process. All of these skills and attributes are needed in order to survive the classroom. I figured my master's of education coursework adequately prepared me to do just about everything I would need to do as a teacher, from how to develop a positive relationship with students to creating dynamic lesson plans to student teaching in a low-income section of San Jose, California. Yet, I don't recall any of my professors teaching a lesson on how to work with controlling and unsupportive administrators, or how to motivate unmotivated students, or how to face challenging discipline problems. To this day, the typical teacher spends many hours preparing lessons before or after contract hours, coming to school on the weekends, taking professional courses on Saturdays, and correcting papers on their weekends. Now what kind of life is that? I was led to believe that I would be teaching paradigmatical students whose learning styles and academic levels were very close to their grade level, was I in for a great surprise.

Today the teacher shortage continues, with a high percentage of new teachers exiting after five years. Educational experts (Ingersoll, 2002; Smith and Ingersoll, 2003) report that nationally, approximately 15 percent of new teachers will leave the teaching profession within the first year, while an alarming 30 percent will make it only to their third year, and 40 to 50 percent will leave the profession within five years. According to the *Alliance for Excellent Education* (Aug. 2005), the cost of replacing teachers leaving the profession is just as staggering as the percent leaving: roughly $7.3 billion a year is lost to teacher abandonment. Even more important is the cost to the students directly affected. They lose out as a result of hiring teachers who are inadequately prepared to teach other people's children. In addition, teachers who are not prepared to teach often lack skills in teaching complex strategies to students—teaching students how to think on a higher level. In addition, they frequently fail to show knowledge of how to reach unmotivated students, skills in managing the classroom, or discipline procedures. Finally, they often lack skill in adapting instruction to different learning styles, especially for students from diverse ethnic groups. Teacher retention is a complex issue; it's an issue akin to a ticking bomb ready to explode. With voices of frustration, irritation, and disgust teachers across the country share their discontent with the teaching profession.

The first teacher states: "I've read books, taken professional development classes, and sweated through staff developments, where I had to meander through classroom management strategies, or what the presenter called classroom management. Despite this, I still felt unsure about my ability to manage my class. There were behavioral problems, but neither the dean or principle supported me." I remember a time when my students were having guided reading time. I didn't know how to convince two students, who refused to participate in guided reading, to read and not disturb the other students. My relationship with my principal isn't the best; he's so text anxious that he puts stress on the teachers. I get no support with my disciplinary problems. I'm so frustrated and ready to quit.

A second teacher expresses her deep concern as a teacher: "As a fourth-year teacher, I've had no mentoring, no constructive feedback and gotten no appreciation from my administrator. Is this a litany of signs coming from above?"

Finally, this writer asserts, "I'm frustrated after five years of teaching. My first year of teaching was frightening; I spent countless hours after school, on weekends doing lessons, prepping, scoring, planning, and generally organizing the classroom. After five years, I am frustrated with the principal, who shows no appreciation, is insecure about his job, and is resentful toward others. I wish there were a class that teaches teachers how to handle difficult administrators, undisciplined students, and the political side of teaching."

There's nothing like a good old fable to offer an explanation for some phenomena. *The Kind Lion and Brave Mouse* by Robert Krause (1994), adds insight into what it's like to step into an unfamiliar situation, into a lion's den. There was a lion that caught a little mouse, with the intent of enjoying a good meal. The profusely sweating, scrawny, terrified mouse begged the huge, powerful lion not to eat him, promising to save him one day should he get in a bind. The lion couldn't imagine a small lion helping him at any time. But, out of the kindness of his heart he let the mouse go. Some time had passed when the lion found himself facing the barrel of a hunter's shotgun. As he stood facing the end of his life, out of nowhere appeared the tiny mouse. Well, the mouse, scaring around looking food, didn't realize the lion was facing danger. Suddenly the mouse ran right in the path and took the bullet, falling on its back. The crying lion ran over to the mouse and wept. The mouse turned over, and with one eye open began to console the lion. The mouse urges the lion not to cry as he was wearing a bullet proof vest and his life was spared. Here's the lesson. Dress as though you're going into a lion's den when facing a new situation.

Reflecting back on my first nine-month position as a teacher at the Brownwood State Home and School, I came to the conclusion that I, too, needed a bulletproof vest, or maybe a mouse, because I was about to step into a lion's den.

The first day of school finally arrived. The textbooks, research, and classes had not prepared me for teaching in the way an actual classroom experience would. I certainly did not know what to expect, especially considering the types of students I would be teaching. There were so many thoughts racing through my mind: *What do I say to these students? What should I do on Monday? How do I conceal my fear? How do I respond to disciplinary problems? Is this what I really want to do?* I drove my old Ford to my new school.

"Hey teacher, where you want us to sit?" shouted a short, dark-haired student. He could not have been more than eleven. I responded with, "You may sit wherever you like for the week." I was about to make my premiere appearance as a teacher. As I surveyed the students, I noticed not too much difference between these students and students in a traditional school setting. They were neatly dressed, in uniforms. The boys' sharply pressed pants stood at attention, and their starched shirts made their chests appear larger than they were. These students were wards of the Brown County Court System. They were not candidates for outstanding citizenship awards; the students housed in this facility had experienced the consequences of behavior problems in a *big* way. There are times in the life of a teacher when you choose not to believe something that actually did happen, not wanting the incident to influence how others perceived that person.

For example, Mark prided himself on his good looks. He stood all of four feet, five and a half inches short. He had compelling blue eyes, a wide, boyish smile, and a pale white face that glistened with innocence. He would not have hurt a fly. But, what Mark did was more than swat a fly. Mark usually entered the class with a "Hello, Mrs. Washington," and an eagerness to do his reading assignment. The other students were no match for Mark. Mark had an incredible enthusiasm for school. He was the type of student any teacher would love to have as a student: respectful to others, helpful to his peers, academically responsible, and so well behaved that he kept other students in line.

Some weeks passed before I got up the courage to ask Mark why he was at this school. His response knocked my off my feet: "My father and I were on our yearly deer-hunting trip when my father yelled at me because I missed for the second time with the deer directly in my path. He often yelled at me and called me stupid. I guess it just got to me and while he was getting ready to make a shot, I moved to the back of him and shot his head off." I cringed with fear, not knowing how to respond, as Mark stood in silence and I sat quietly, wondering what my next words should be. Taking a deep breath, exhaling slowly, counting to ten, and calming myself, I reluctantly asked for the details.

There were plenty of discipline problems, even though there was an armed security guard on every hall. I was determined not to show my fear in handling these discipline problems. I was about to get on-the-job training in classroom management. One Monday, four boys had not finished a fight that had begun in their cottage, and decided to end their dispute on the school grounds. Moving confidently, I continued my daily morning routine of taking attendance, checking for completed homework, and making certain the students were in their assigned centers. Suddenly, the room felt threatening, discordantly tense, and strained. Something was brewing; I could feel it. Now would be a perfect time to show the principal that I knew very well how to resolve discipline problems. I had to quickly come up with a reactive discipline plan. The proactive side of management had been addressed; the physical setting, discipline procedures, and setting the cognitive environment. Now, I needed to act on a plan. Thus I calmly responded to the four boys by remind them that if they acted on their threats to one another it would jeopardize their chances of leaving the school. Doing this allowed the boys to save their reputations, as most of the high school students were raring to get back to their home school. In the end, we all laughed about the situation. Humor counts for something.

Going back I remember that my three and a half years of teaching at the Brownwood State Home and School prepared me for what lay ahead in my teaching career: The need for classroom discipline strategies, more focused lesson plans, engaging lesson activities, rethinking my instructional plans, and developing an eye for identifying the reluctant and unmotivated learner. But my first teacher observation, in 1974, indicated that I needed help in being a stronger disciplinarian. If I weren't a person who believes in winning, I would have walked right out of the teaching profession. I was evaluated on a scale of one to five, with five being the highest, on more than thirty general characteristics the principal felt every teacher should have. A sample follows: Initiative, ambition, potential, motivation, creativity, communication, ability to solve problems, job knowledge, stamina, cooperation/courtesy, productivity, creativity, promptness, personal appearance, and discipline. What a frightening evaluation; that came from a principal who spelled "too," as in "too little motivation," as "to" in three summaries.

I knew that even though I had planned to the "ninth" for any foreseeable behavioral problems, I wasn't able to catch them all. As time went along I just got better at being a stronger disciplinarian and knowing how to recognize problems before a situation turns physical.

An Angel in Sagging Blue Jeans

All students can learn.

—*Christopher Morley*

I had just begun my contractual year with the Clark County School District, and my first year, I was given a fifth-grade teaching assignment at an elementary school in Henderson. The school was located in an older, lower socio-economic area of town. There were approximately 60 percent white, 25 percent black, and 15 percent Hispanic students. I was so excited, eager, motivated, and ready to go. The students were just as excited about being in my class as I was about having them. The fact that I was the only black teacher on campus, actually the only black teacher in Henderson, didn't seem to bother them. Daily, the students greeted me with smiling faces and bright eyes; I really felt that being a teacher was going to be just great. Fears, worries, concerns never once entered my mind. Many teachers worry about maintaining classroom discipline; it is the biggest fear for most new teachers and is a skill that has to be learned on a daily basis through trial and error. Little did I know that one of my students would soon disrupt my classroom's learning environment.

At the beginning of the first semester of the school year, the principal began transferring a large number of students into my room. I really didn't give it much thought until my class count became a point of conversation in the teacher's lounge. All eyes were on me as I mentioned how frustrated I was with the large number of students in my class, All heads dropped, teachers began to scatter, and eyes rolled.

One would have thought that a rattler had hit the table. There I was, sitting all alone, only later to see what was happening. I realized that the white fourth- and fifth-grade teachers were transferring students who had behavioral problems into my class. I worked hard to meet the diverse academic needs. I was determined to beat the odds until I had to face a serious discipline problem.

To this day, I can see Sylvia's tall demeanor, tough, massive broad shoulders, hear her thundering voice, and feel a tense energy fill the classroom. Sylvia was not the typical fifth-grade student. She was tall for her age, five-feet-seven, hefty, wide-boned, and well acquainted with street life. She wore blue jeans most of the time. I don't believe Sylvia knew what a smile was, as I don't recall her ever smiling. Her dark hair was closely napped and her skin was brittle, perhaps because it was dry. Sylvia's tone of voice was deep, almost like a bass tone. I had high hopes for her, even thinking, "Maybe she will go on to community college," while other teachers saw Sylvia going on to juvenile hall followed by jail. Way deep down inside of Sylvia was a better being. Sylvia expressed her pain through profanity, fighting, and poor academic performance. She wore sagging blue jeans. Her nature was rather lethal and there were students and teachers who were intimidated by her presence. There wasn't a teacher on campus who wanted the likes of her in their classroom; she had been transferred out two fifth-grade teachers' classes. Now it was my turn to have her in my class. Sylvia came from a rough household and lived in a housing project. I knew that she often carried a pocketknife for protection. Her mom and dad were products of the penal system, and several of her siblings had been in the juvenile detention system. Sylvia hated herself because of her family life. I could understand and sympathize with her dislike for school, as she had never experienced any success there, never received praise or even a kind word. I didn't do much to make her feel positive about her academic performance or anything else. I did place her in a group with students who were good academic performers.

Sylvia was really a harmless child who needed someone to stand up to her, love her, and mentor her. Reaching Sylvia would take time, patience, and the involvement of her parents. What was about to happen was unimaginable in a public school; I expected a problem with student unrest at the state school, but not an elementary school.

It was a November day when the weather had just begun to cool down. The fall day was bright and beautiful; the sun was not too warm, a relief from the long hot summer, and the breeze ran softly across our faces. Sylvia entered the room late, as was her custom. Today would not be a good day for her. I positioned myself in one of the reading circles as I prepared to direct them in the day's reading lesson, while the other reading groups were busily engaged in their small group exercises. About an hour into our reading group, Sylvia blurted to another student, "You don't like it, do something about it!" I eyed the class's response and then looked at Sylvia. Her posture clearly said *Hit me; I dare you.* In my most demanding tone of voice, I told Sylvia, "Take your seat *now!*" Sylvia retorted, "Make me."

I was not ready for that response. I went over to Sylvia and attempted to quiet her when, without warning, she bristled at me. So that no other student would be harmed, I dismissed my class, with their lessons in hand, and instructed them to complete their assignment outside. They quietly exited the room. Sylvia and I were left standing confrontationally alone. She continued to "loudmouth" me. I proceeded to place chairs against the wall, not sure of what Sylvia's plan was, what she might have been thinking. I prepared myself for the unknown. My heart was pounding like hands beating upon a drum, yet I knew I had to be vigilant. Sylvia's dark, fiery eyes pierced me as though she were a cannon ready to fire at any moment. She raised her hands, fists folded. I quickly reminded her that she was in violation of the district's behavioral policy, threatening to bring bodily harm to a teacher. She began to express words of hate for teachers at the school and for her young life. It was clear that Sylvia felt that she had nothing to lose by inflicting physical harm upon me. Instead of challenging her physically or verbally, I chose to use words that expressed my care for her. I told Sylvia that I believed in her and that she was capable of accomplishing whatever she put her hands and head to doing, no matter what others said about her. I asked her to forgive me for not being sensitive to her hurt, pain, and lack of success in my class. Here might have been another reason to run, not walk, out of the profession, but I was determined to make a difference in the young life of one of my students.

It became very clear Sylvia had no security at home or at school. A sense of security is really the first thing that students need in order to feel that they will still be accepted if they fail. They feel comfortable that if they ask questions, they will get responses that aren't judgmental.

The incident with Sylvia was the beginning of a new training ground for me.

To build a sense of security for Sylvia, I first sought to build trust. Trust is a psychological security that all of us need. It stems from the home environment, and carries over into school. For children, trust is knowing that their parents can be depended on, that they are consistent, and that they behave responsibly. I understand why Sylvia felt as she did about her home life. Trusting at the school level meant that Sylvia needed to see that I trusted her; she could put her faith in me, as she saw that I was dependable and had her best interests in mind. The initial trust came when Sylvia shared information about her home life. Even though her secret was shared publicly, it was meant to be private. A second ingredient to security is honesty. I began to practice honesty with Sylvia. Sylvia was probably used to adults not being honest with her, hiding the facts that she lacked academic skills and had weak interpersonal skills; she was not likely to be chosen as the "most liked student" on campus.

To put trust and honesty into practice, I created a situation. I allowed Sylvia to do such things as run errands to the office, set the listening center up, and be in charge of passing out the PE equipment. I cannot believe how much allowing her to do these little projects lifted her spirits and built her trust in me.

Although we had classroom rules, boundaries, expectations, and consequences, students were not often reminded or admonished for neglecting to follow them. Our classroom rules were well defined. We had rules that defined expected classroom behavior, rules that defined procedures, rules that defined the rights and responsibilities of students. However, the one rule that was not carefully explained was the one defining rights and responsibilities. So, I rewrote the rule, adding an example, prohibiting ridiculing the way other students dress, name-calling, or teasing because of speech, ideas, feelings. Students were also warned about using inappropriate language, fighting, and being disrespectful to adults.

Next, I taught myself how not to censure students personally, in order to keep embarrassments down; this would keep students from becoming defensive. Believe me, Sylvia would frequently become defensive when I stated, "Sylvia, why are you again out of your seat? I'm not going to tell you again to stay in your seat." I know I'm not the only teacher who does/did that. I changed my language to "Sylvia, I know what you're doing is important, but I really need you to take a seat. Thanks."

Sylvia soon began to work and play cooperatively with other students. I consistently gave words of encouragement, listened to her, and provided her with opportunities to work within the class community, to lead, to work with a partner, and to be a teacher helper. She soon recovered. Other students on campus noticed a difference, as did other teachers.

As May approached, my students were aware of my impending move to another school. I overheard whispers about presents and flowers; my students knew I loved flowers. I didn't expect my students to give me anything, even though they seemed to enjoy giving gifts. My Sylvia, the leader of the pack, managed to quietly organize a surprise party. The entire event was staged as "Queen for a Day." Somehow, Sylvia rounded up gobs of flowers. I don't know where she got them; maybe she had a florist donate day-old flowers. In any case, they were all beautiful. Each student presented a gift, believing it was the best .What a great way to end my elementary school teaching career.

Overall, most students engage in some form of misbehavior; they talk while you are instructing, hit other students, tease or bully, and even become sarcastic with teachers. There are reasons students misbehave. Some misbehave because they don't like school or your class, some misbehave out of boredom, some simply have yet to experience any academic success. Most teachers have a plan for less serious misbehaviors, but nothing in place for serious behavior offenders. In C.M. Charles's 2005 analysis of Curwin and Mendler's *Discipline with Dignity* (1992), Charles asserts that there are students who know the rules for appropriate conduct and break them anyway as a means of "gaining a measure of control over a system that has damaged their sense of dignity." Teachers see this when a student argues, talks back, gets in a teacher's face, or even taps a pencil or drops books. But students' belligerence can also be seen when the student becomes insubordinate or continually engages in other overt type inappropriate behaviors. These students look for other students with similar attitudes. Beware, they can potentially wreck a good lesson. By the way, never turn your back on your class; if you leave room for commotion, pandemonium is bound to result.

As teachers, we face angels in sagging jeans daily. Yes, these types of students make teaching frustrating—the very thing that runs new teachers out the door. But there are steps teachers can take to deal with serious misbehaviors. How teachers respond to students determines the level of the teacher-student relationship. The first order of business for me is to create learning environments that are respectful, supportive, stimulating, and encouraging. Mendler and Curwin (1999) suggest that teachers begin with the idea of helping the student regain hope, something we all need to achieve success in some form. This is accomplished by making the learning activity purposeful, meaningful, and something students can relate to. This works! For example, take a reading assignment and read a story they can relate to. As an English teacher, I found this challenging. I had to find an enrichment story and build an English assignment around it. It worked, but again, it was challenging and tiring. Next, make the lesson one in which the student can experience some measure of success, without diminishing credibility by minimizing the purpose of the lesson: the thinking, writing, and creating skills. Next, give positive "I" messages, or pats on the shoulder. The "I" message is a powerful way of bringing respect, encouragement, and approval to the learning environment and recognizing positive discipline. Allow the problem students to interact, with their own values, habits, attitudes. You might consider making those students group leaders, allowing them to take risks and make decisions. At the end of class, be sure you give the students with behavioral problems positive acclamations. Be sure to reiterate consequences for misbehavior. Stand firm. Do not argue or make a deal with a student. Be an active listener, and by all means, document all student behaviors, both acceptable and unacceptable. Finally, show your interest in the success of the student.

Did You Hear What
Johnny Called the Teacher?

I see the mind of a five-year-old as a volcano with two vents: destructiveness and creativeness.

—Sylvia Ashton-Warner

You know the feeling of handling a challenging behavior problem in your classroom. New teachers may feel intimidated or fearful or may lack confidence in disciplining a student. For example, envision a new teacher attempting to discipline a senior student who is robust, full of himself, and wants to show off; suddenly he gets in the teacher's face. As that teacher, you may ask yourself, "Should I send for help from the office?" or "Should I APOS (alternative placement of student) the student? What should I do if he yells at me?" These are common questions plaguing new and veteran teachers. That's a trap students set up for teachers. I will always have vivid memories of a select group of students in my eighth-grade English class at Biltmore Opportunity School—a large class. Students at alternative schools are there because of their inappropriate behavior. I like the idea of documenting specific behaviors students should be working on in order to measure their progress; this really helps when student evaluation time comes. These particular students were known to be the worst students on campus. "Dr. Lindsey, we're going to add nine new students to your eighth-grade English class," the school counselor said. His voice sounded apologetic, as though he was feeling sorry for me. I had learned that occasionally there were students who would test my ability to handle classroom

35

discipline or test the waters of what was acceptable behavior and what would not be tolerated.

Well acquainted with classroom procedures, I initiated the normal steps to begin any new school year. First, I established classroom policies alongside their consequences. I always highlighted the most important policies with actual examples. Going over the classroom and school policies, not rules, is never an easy task, as students don't see the necessity for policies. The policies Biltmore had were sufficient for managing the school, but not the classroom. For example, you will agree that not many students like being told what they can and cannot wear. Imagine girls being told they can't wear skirts and the boys being told they can't wear pants that sag. Having to look at a boy's underwear is not appealing to most teachers or conducive to the appropriate classroom environment.

The second major concern was the use of profanity in the classroom. Students today spend more than forty hours a week watching television, and more than half of what they see includes profanity. In addition, parents and adult household members have their own lists of unsuitable words. Studies on the use of profanity attribute this increase to the lack of adequate language acquisition, a problem with its own separate causes.

Let's be real. It would be unlikely to find a teacher who gets along with every student in the class. Butting heads with students in the classroom is not unusual. It comes from differences in beliefs, values, policies, or opinions; it may happen because students insist on having their own way. With that in mind, the third element was to make sure my students understand rule number three: "Respect for your teacher is expected in this class." Lack of respect was the main problem that landed students at Biltmore. Students came to us for such problems as being insubordinate, fighting, brandishing a weapon, threatening a teacher, excessively using inflammatory language toward a teacher, striking a teacher, or using alcohol or drugs on campus. I always believed that Biltmore teachers were expected to "work miracles."

In an alternative environment, a teacher's first priority is classroom management. The teacher's role is disciplinarian first and teacher second. Unlike the traditional school where your students test your patience, kindness, and firmness the first day of the week, in the alternative school, students test you daily. The purpose of alternative schools is to help students identify alternative positive behaviors. Eventually, students were placed back in the traditional school setting based on their behavior, attendance, and grades.

Hecklers can easily turn an orderly classroom environment topsy-turvy. Johnny was such a student. He was a disrupter who encouraged other students to disrupt: He interrupted others, made personal comments about me to the class, single-handedly and deliberately interrupted instruction, yelled across the room, and was sometimes successful in enticing other students to buy into his plan to destroy the classroom with outbursts. Working with him was like working with three students at the same time.

I have worked with students who exhibited diverse types of neurotic behavior, such as suddenly yelling out, hitting their heads on the desk, and breaking pencils, but Johnny was unique. He was a student seemingly filled with so much pain, hurt, and anger that it caused him to break out into sudden disruptive and hostile behavior. Johnny's short, stocky body accentuated his tough, devilish look. Johnny looked as if he lifted weights to build up his wide shoulders and rangy body. Johnny's evil smile spread across his thick lips, and the dark, angry expression on his face left me believing that Johnny was an unhappy student. He would slowly stroll into class, engaging in short conversation and laughter with his peers. I always felt that Johnny was telling them of his plot to disturb the class. Johnny knew the classroom policies, but following them was another issue.

On one occasion, I told Johnny to pull his sagging pants up because his underwear was showing. He responded, "Wanna see more?" Now why would Johnny even so much as think I'd want to see more of him? He proceeded to pull them up, but not without some drama. In one step, Johnny went from dress violation to disrupting class instruction. When I told him this would be the last time I would warn him to stop annoying others, Johnny lashed out. "You're tripping, man," he yelled. "Shut up, you ain't talkin' to no child!" Finally, he said, "I'm gonna have my mom come up here and whip you, since I can't." His eyes penetrated mine with vicious hate. Johnny then began to heave his upper torso, bristling up as though preparing to attack me. I learned from my first year of teaching not to show shock, anger, or embarrassment. Instead, I kept my cool, even joking about his gesture.

I relaxed my face, but my heart raced, as did my mind. "Lord, please hold this child's anger or prepare me for whatever is about to happen."

This was a student I constantly had to keep watch over, because Johnny's behavior was always a problem. It was clear to see that Johnny had experienced neither positive attention nor success in life. His obscene gestures resulted in a referral, and Johnny was suspended for two days. I actually felt sorry for Johnny. Here was a student who was familiar with rejection. I usually let him know that his behavior was not appreciated, which was a show of rejection. I often removed him from the class setting, another form of rejection. At one point, I even butted heads with Johnny by using a "dare" tactic on him. I had to clearly articulate to the class rules about being subordinate, and the consequences. Here was a student in desperate need of counseling. He was not capable of effectively functioning in an academic setting, or any other setting; here was a student who had no social skills, a loss of academic skills, and a disappointing family life. This was one student I was not able to reach. The interventions I used were parent conferences and student documentation. Unfortunately, the conferences were not positive; Johnny's mother said, "I don't know what to do with him. His dad is in jail and he has already told me he wants to be like his dad, even if it means going to jail." The counselor, principal, and I were all dumbfounded, simply at a loss for words. We concluded that Johnny should be placed on a behavior contract requiring that he get each teacher to document his behavior and academic performance every day. Johnny agreed on the precise behaviors that needed adjusting and agreed to make the change. His mother simply nodded and said, "I hope this will keep him out of juvie or jail; he wants a car."

To teach in an alternative school, you have to be firm and undaunted to survive. You must make certain your students know, without a doubt and from the start, that you are the boss in that classroom. And you must constantly remind them; you don't want them to forget. Sometimes I think alternative students, or students with persistent behavioral problems, plot and premeditate their crimes, even though they seem to be spontaneous with their misbehavior. For example: Kathleen thought she knew how to push my buttons.

Kathleen was capable of preventing me from moving on with my instruction and cheating on an assignment, she preferred being a teacher's aide to doing class work. I was certainly not the teacher to pull this one on. I could read this girl like a book. Kathleen and I had frequent clashes because she not only tried to con teachers, but also had problems with authority figures. She was strong-willed and arrogant, had an uncontrollable temper, disrespected herself and others, was manipulative, and used a lot of profanity. Kathleen's trim, simple, but well-groomed gold hair highlighted her petite and flawless body. Her complexion was blemished, like the typical junior high school student's, but pleasant to look at. Even though Kathleen could be a terror, her smile was warm and echoed in her voice. On the flip side, Kathleen's pleasant smile was capable of becoming unpleasantly twisted. She would frown with cold fury and her mouth would form into an even deeper frown. She did not see herself as having any problems. According to Kathleen, it was not her fault that she was in Opportunity; it was the teacher's fault.

There are students who would rather write notes than do a lesson activity. Such was the case with Kathleen. There were plenty of times when I didn't feel up to teaching paragraph writing, and I understood when a student didn't want to write. It just seems that you have to be in the right frame of mind when you write. I suppose Kathleen was never in the right frame of mind to write or complete homework assignments. Students were told to exchange homework papers so that they could be graded as a teacher-guided activity. I thought that all students were following along, but as I walked around the room, I saw that Kathleen was not working on a peer paper but writing a note. She did not notice me silently standing and watching her. In a quiet and sincere manner, I unobtrusively tapped her on her shoulder and motioned for her to quickly and quietly step to the corner of the room. This is a second strategy I use to handle discipline concerns before they get out of hand. She complied. I knew that she hadn't done the homework, yet I was hoping to be wrong. Kathleen became argumentative. "Kathleen," I responded, "you did not turn your paper." I didn't make a big deal out of the note writing, even though that is a pet peeve of mine.

Kathleen yelled, "You're full of bull crap. You are a friggin' liar." Now, she was expressing anger, and there was need for me to go to strategy three: a private moment. In a calm, respectful, concerned tone of voice, I told Kathleen to go outside the room and wait for me to have a private moment with her. The other students could not hear my request. She heaved with anger. Kathleen could be the most positive student in her classes, but she could quickly turn up the volume on her soft-spoken voice. There were times I excused Kathleen to chill out and times when I referred her to the office. I eased into the empty student desk next to

Kathleen and chatted with her about the current assignment, offering to assist her. To show Kathleen that I was a concerned teacher, I reminded her of previous assignments that were well done. Kathleen asked to redo the assignment in question. I reminded her of my expectation and our classroom discipline and work ethic. At this point, I needed to assess the type of disruptive behavior. Disruptive classroom behavior comes in two forms: behavior that directly interferes with classroom instruction and behavior that is directed at the instructor. Clearly, Kathleen's behavior was directed at me. This type of behavior surely interferes with instruction, but is in direct violation of most, if not all, codes of conduct for any educational institution. Believing something else was behind this outburst, I took the situation to another level, getting the parents and school counselor involved (Griffith, 2009).

Kathleen's mother entered the picture after our third encounter. This conference centered around her insubordinate behavior, extreme use of profanity, disrespect of authority, uncontrollable temper tantrums, and leaving the class without permission. Her mother was very supportive, stating that Kathleen often acted in a similar manner at home. I do believe Kathleen intended to set me up as a liar so that her mom would take her side. It didn't work. Kathleen lost control by displaying her typical behavior—temper tantrums and outbursts—behaviors that interfered with the flow of the parent conference. Kathleen needed to vent her anger against her parents, teacher, school, friends, and life. We allowed her to cry as she shared it all. Exhausted, Kathleen slumped back into her chair, took a deep breath, and sat silently. None of us spoke for a couple of minutes; we needed to let Kathleen's concerns soak in. Finally, I took the floor. In my most reassuring, compassionate, loving spirit and tone, I lightly touched Kathleen's hand and let her know I heard her concerns, appreciated her sharing her deepest thoughts, and was willing to be a support system for her. We discussed ways she felt I could support her and still be her teacher.

Kathleen had a wealth of academic talent and creativity, but she obviously chose to take the wrong road—destruction. She needed more order in her life and one of the ways to get it was to face her problematic behaviors and begin making wise choices. Kathleen, along with the school counselor, developed a behavioral contract, which helped keep her on track.

3. GETTING IT TOGETHER

"A man must know his destiny ... if he does not recognize it, then he is lost."

— George S. Patton

"Your classroom management techniques work in practice but not in theory. That worries me."

Monday, Monday

On a good day, I view the job of president as directing an orchestra. On the dark days, it is more like that of a clutch—engaging the engine to effect forward motion, while taking greater friction.

— *A. Bartlett Giamatti*

One beautiful, sunny day while enjoying the beach, I became intrigued with teenage surfers. Each wave that came up was different; a small one would be followed by a giant wave. The boys seemed to enjoy the challenge of surfing the giant, robust waves. Now, I don't surf, but I could tell they had a strategy for riding out the waves. First, they decided which wave was a good one to ride. Next, they had to determine how to hold onto the wave. Finally, they had to decide how they would ride out the wave. Surfing reminds me of the turbulent waves Mondays can bring. I suppose it's how well you prepare to ride the rough wave that matters. It reminds me of a wonderfully written fable called "The Opihi's Strength" by Leslie Ann Hayashi, in *Fables From the Sea* (2002), that reads:

"Today, children, we'll venture to the water's edge," the father of 'opihi told his five children. Lined up in a row, they formed a small string of tiny gray striped volcanoes along the top of the rocks, not far from the breakwater. "Fasten yourselves to the rocks just below the tide's edge. When the ocean recedes, continue to hold on until the waves return."

"How long will that be?"

"Usually, it's just a few hours."

"What if we get tired, Daddy? Or scared?"

"Or hungry?" The littlest one always thought about food.

43

"The tide must reach its lowest point before it returns. But it always returns. The most important thing to remember is to hold on. No matter what happens, you must never let go."

Little did the father 'opihi know that a large storm was quickly approaching. Before the father could get his family firmly situated on the rocks, the storm's dark clouds blotted out the warm sun. Unleashing its fury, the storm sent waves crashing with great might against the rocks, dislodging crabs and fish from their safe resting places. "Quick, children, attach yourself to the rocks and don't let go!" the father shouted as the first wave crashed over them.

After that, only the pounding of the surf could be heard. Wave after wave crashed upon the shore with tremendous force and energy. The ocean and the sky twisted together, forming one large silver-gray mass that churned everywhere in its path. By morning, the turbulent waves gradually subsided. The ocean regained its shining smooth surface. Thick, dark clouds dispersed before the brilliant light of the sun. Debris lay strewn on the rocks and along the beach. Uprooted trees bobbed in the water. As the tide receded, there was the 'opihi family still firmly fastened to the rocks, safe and sound!

Mondays in all walks of life are hectic and usually full of pressure. You brace yourself for whatever Monday brings. That's why on any given Friday, you will likely hear "Thank goodness it's Friday" as your colleagues retreat to a place where they can relax and unwind. A bad Monday can throw your entire workweek into havoc. For example, you run from one copy machine to another trying to copy worksheets for today, only to discover that all four of them are down. So off you go to the graphic arts room, hoping the graphic arts person is there, and you beg to have copies made. Then, you scramble back to your room only to find that your lesson plans need adjusting because you've just heard from a colleague that each class period today has been shortened by fifteen minutes; you failed to read the e-mail announcing the shortened classes. Oh no, just as you begin to rewrite your lesson plan for Monday, your name is called over the intercom: "Dr. Lindsey, your 7:30 parent conference is in the counselor's office." "What parent conference? I do not know anything about a parent conference." You then discover that the counselor scheduled a Monday parent conference without notifying you. And so it goes. You cannot plan for Monday on a Monday morning.

Many teachers new to teaching come with strong content or subject-matter knowledge, but have no idea of how to write effective pedagogical plans. After some time in the profession, teachers realize that having content knowledge plays a much smaller role in their success or failure as a teacher than they initially understood. It is true that content knowledge is extremely important. However, how students come to know and understand the content is more important. Current research now focuses on how knowledge comes to be known. There are several important strategies for writing great lesson plans that will yield great classrooms. The initial groundwork needs to be done—being aware of the demographics, learning abilities, age, and reading levels. Once that is done, the teacher has a paved avenue by which to plan engaged activities or exercises, and the type of assignments that will increase metacognition, enhance awareness of students' learning styles, improve attitudes about learning and decision-making, and, in the end, improve students' academic performance. Let's talk about lesson plan strategies.

First, define the objective of the lesson, and the steps the class will take to meet the objective. Your objective should clearly say what your students will be able to do as a result of the lesson. For example, students will comprehend the details of the story and identify what a story is mainly about by reading a short text. How easy is that? Your lesson plan should be set up in a similar manner. Design your lesson plan so that it echoes your district's content and develops mental standards.

Second, set the stage for learning. Setting the stage is of the utmost importance for your lesson. You would not want to go to a play and not know the plot until near the end. Your procedures tell what the teacher will do to help students reach the objectives and standards. The lesson plan must be so creative that it gets the students' attention and piques their interest throughout the lesson. For example, you might consider showing a short clip of the central idea; how about having the students respond to a bell ringer or warm-up? Maybe you could introduce the lesson by having the students respond in writing to an open prompt. This is important to your lesson formulation. Once the objective has been defined in your lesson plans, you now need to list the kinds of skills and activities that your students will engage in. Your lesson should include Bloom's Taxonomy. The taxonomy was created by Benjamin Bloom in 1956. It categorizes different levels of reasoning skills. There are actually six levels in the taxonomy: knowledge, comprehension, application, analysis, synthesis, and application. The knowledge level addresses your students' comprehension of what has been taught. For example, how well do they recall dates, events, or characters? The comprehension level requires that your students show that they understand the information. So you'll want your questions to use such words as describe, contrast, compare, discuss, and predict. The application process requires students to actually apply, or use the knowledge they have acquired. Students will be told to create a solution to a problem, so you'll want to use words like complete, solve, examine, illustrate, or show. The analysis level encourages students to analyze, explain, investigate, or infer something about what has been learned. As your students' thinking increases, they will soon be able to synthesize what has been learned. To synthesize means students use given facts to create new theories or make predictions. Your lesson plans will include words like invent, imagine, create, compose. Finally, the evaluation level requires students to assess information by judging, debating, recommending, or determining the value or bias of something learned.

Once you have explained the concepts and provided the necessary illustrations, you will need to make certain you note where students will work independently; that's where guided instruction/practice comes in. For example, your lesson plans might involve students in a small group-writing activity; maybe have them participate in a discussion about the subject, explore, or experiment with the topic at their own pace. All of these strategies should be briefly noted in your lesson plans. Make sure you plan for classroom management.

Third, your lesson plans must assess student learning. This is where you see if the lesson was taught effectively; this can be done in a couple of ways: observing students working, assigning application activities, getting feedback, using out-the-door questioning, or even having students complete a short-answer pop quiz. It is time to discuss their work, discuss what they have learned, and encourage the subject matter.

Finally, your lesson plans must show modifications and accommodations for any special-needs students in the class.

Here's how I usually welcomed a typical Monday morning. I knew there were many tasks I needed to do before the first bell rang. I've got forty-five minutes before the first class begins. The first thing I notice upon entering my room are the scads of composition papers in my work area. I can't get to my desk for the mounds of student papers that still need to be either graded or recorded. I'll just move them onto the floor behind my desk, this way they won't be visible. As I look behind my desk I notice there are papers already on the floor; well I'll just have to make room for more papers. Ah, ah, I'll stick them in the corner near the computer desk although that may be a problem accessing my computer; besides, there are papers stacked on top of the printer, and sticky notes around the computer screen. I finally check messages in my computer. "What's this?" I have a pre-evaluation during my prep period. "Oh, no, I really need that time to organize my desk."

I need to check and make sure all materials are laid out and that there are enough for all students. I'll use the worksheet as guided independent practice or as a small group activity. That will certainly maintain classroom management. Oh, no. Friday I gave the materials that I needed copied for this week to graphic arts, and they were not in my mailbox this morning. I'll need to call down to the graphic arts room and see if the worksheets are ready, and then make a quick run down there. "Nicky, do you have some student worksheets ready for me to pick up?" "No, you didn't leave anything with me Dr. Lindsey." Where are those student papers? I must have left them in the department chair's room. I'll have to see if Nicky has time to run ninety copies that will get me through the first three class periods. Not much time. I'll need to change from my high heels and put on my flats and run.

I now have ten minutes to re-read my lesson plans, set out the short end of the lesson assessment, and set the tone for learning. I know the lesson can be measured in a number of ways; assigning application activities, getting verbal feedback, use a out the door questioning, even having students complete a short answer pop quiz. Today, I think I'll allow students to complete an out-the-door exercise. It consists of three questions multiple choice, fill-in-the blank, and one short answer. Students will hand in their papers on the way out.

Finally, I need to put tonight's homework on the board. There's the 8:00 a.m. bell, just as I finish the putting the last word on the homework board. There's still time to greet students at the door, who are passing into my class. I usually have stragglers; they're not excited about getting to an English class. My tardy clip board is in place, and I always keep my tardy paper work handy for students who are tardy, taking care of tardies is a routine. As students enter the classroom, I urge them to use the last few minutes to take of bathroom needs, as I don't give bathroom passes. That rule has cut down on the misuse of bathroom privilege. Students are also reminded to prepare mentally by reading and jotting down the lesson objective, the warm-up exercise, writing the homework in their daily planner, making a line for parent signature, and getting rid of their gum. I do a dress code check as I greet students, and remind students to sharpen pencils.

I began my first period class with the usual routine, the warm-up or essential question(s) that really is a review from a previous lesson. Today I decide to roam the room as a means of taking attendance. This way I get to speak to each student and see how they are responding to the opening activity. I allowed students about six minutes to complete the opening, sometimes it takes longer. I notice that Carlos and Juan are here today; this means I'll need to be on guard. When these two guys are present their behavior is usually a disturbance. Believe me neither one is the least bit interested in getting an education: Carlos is sixteen years old in the seventh grade, and Juan is fifteen in the seventh grade. As I reach their desk I let them know that I'm expecting them to actively participate today because they are students of excellence. Which they really aren't, both of them are truants and have flunked English for the last two years. This class is a handful. So, I've creatively arranged my student activities. That will minimize and defuse discipline problems.

As the day progresses I realize that I must gather materials for Tuesday's teaching and learning activity—a DVD—and check to make certain my DVD-video player works. I need to remove the student projects off the top of the five student computers so that students are able to use the computers Tuesday.

Mondays used to leave me tired from spending five hours or more making extensive and exhaustive lesson plans. Plotting all those course syllabus numbers, course goals, and objectives and adhering to benchmarks meant spending hours writing lesson plans. Mondays meant standing in high-heeled shoes all day. Standing long hours is something most teachers have to do. Monday meant getting my students' minds engaged; that was the most challenging venture on Mondays.

I have learned, after twenty-eight years of teaching, that I really should be planning for Monday on Friday, even if it means staying ten minutes late. Successful people are organized people. I take additional steps to ensure that my Monday is off and running. "Whew, I'm glad today is over." The last bell rings, students scramble out the door, teachers standing at their door with looks of relief on their faces. Today has passed, but tomorrow is nearby. Friday is coming and yet, another Monday will roll around.

What's Management Got to Do with Anything?

Anticipate, plan, control relax.

— *Greg Henry*

Teachers don't likely think of the learning environment as part of classroom management; yet, it is. I made certain my students received solid instruction, always linking their prior knowledge alongside different enrichment activities. You can't separate management from instruction, the learning environment, classroom policies, and learning activities. A classroom without a conducive learning climate invariably will lead to poor student academic performance. Early research by Duke (1979) defines classroom management as "provisions and procedures necessary to establish and maintain an environment in which instruction and learning occur." When we speak of classroom management, we are not focusing on keeping a room from being chaotic; instead, we are referring to creating a classroom that lends itself to student learning and encourages appropriate behavior.

Teachers, creating a physical environment that is conducive to academic success means you must carefully plan from the start of the school year. If you consider yourself an indispensable unique teacher who knows how to creatively present pedagogy, you don't need a lot of posters, tools, or useless instruments to manage your classroom. What follows are suggestions on how to better manage your classroom.

Let's begin with the teacher's desk. How does a cluttered desk make you feel? What impression does your administrator have on your organizational and management style? What do you think your cluttered desk says about you as a person? It looks bad when a teacher's desk is cluttered: Students' papers from two weeks ago piled high, lesson plan book sitting on your printer, parent notes tucked away on the corner of your desk, a day old can of coke hidden behind your computer, a small camera in sight for students to take, important notes from the recent staff development meeting, and your desk is positioned so that you cannot easily access classroom activities. To begin, consider arranging your desk so that you are able to see every activity in your class. Next, train you eyes to survey the room, even with your head down. Purchasing desk organizers will definitely be beneficial to managing your class. Also don't allow students to congregate around your desk, it's too tempting for them to "lift" items that look interesting. Finally, ladies if you insist on taking your purse into your class lock it up. I've known many ladies who've had their purses stolen right under their nose. This shows a lack of classroom management. I never took my purse into the classroom. Instead I would lock it in the trunk of my car before driving onto the school parking lot.

I've gone into rooms where the bulletin boards are plastered with posters that show very little evidence of what is to be learned, classroom seating is not configured with the room, and rules are written in small words posted without consequences. On the other hand, there is the room where the teacher has created structure, orderliness, where students know what the behavioral policies are and the consequences for disorderly conduct. They also know what learning will take place resulting from instructional bulletin boards. Instructional bulletin boards will illustrate the course objectives, and connect with what the students will learn. Remember, give your boards color, make them fun, and use action words.

In this classroom, learning will take place; it is a well-managed classroom. The challenge is creating a motivational climate for learning and combining it with the physical climate. Believe me, if you don't set the standard for the learning environment in the beginning and try to do such months after school begins, your management will suffer.

A final point on the learning environment is preparing a positive cognitive space so that learning takes place and the class can be managed. Things to consider in preparing for a learning activity include determining a pre-instruction activity, setting expectations, engaging the students, reviewing activity policies, and making sure the teacher's own motivation is high. Begin the school year with a positive emphasis on class learning procedures and rules. Identify clear expectations and consequences. Don't be afraid to use your teacher power; be assertive when needed. Classroom management means allowing for time management of procedures, pacing, and transitions. Next, management includes instruction, guided practices, reviews, and other prerequisites to a lesson. A good classroom manager leaves room in the lesson plans for application, which is teacher feedback and monitoring of the implementation of the skill.

Briefly, the physical environment includes making certain the lighting is good, the room is not too warm or too cold, distractions are at a minimum, the room arrangement prepares students for the learning activity, and materials are available.

As a strong classroom manager, I made certain my students received solid instruction as well as time to connect with what they already know, unfold new information, practice independently, and review. When students did practice assignments, I would allow them to confide in one another. However, I didn't understand the importance of classroom management until much later in my teaching career. Nor did I have knowledge of the principles that guide management: the dynamics of classroom management, including time management, transitions, classroom arrangement, wait time, and wrapping up a lesson.

Sandy continued to look away from me hastily; she restlessly shifted in her seat and her thoughts seemed disconnected from her English class. I noticed that Sandy's eyes darted nervously around the classroom, while her head maintained a bowed position. Small, frail Sandy sat near my desk. She was different from her classmates. Many days, I noticed that her hair was unkempt, her clothes were tattered and not ironed, and she wore worn tennis shoes that flopped on her feet because they appeared to be one size too large. The rancid smell of her body would sometimes leave me nauseated. Although my students were occasionally assigned group work, most of the time they worked independently. As such, their desks were arranged in rows in the traditional manner. On this particular day, I had spent too much time teaching adjectives to a small group of students, unaware that something was brewing in the back of the room. I'd taken my eyes off the class, which typically doesn't happen. Even though my rules guiding acceptable behavior were posted, the consequences for acting irresponsibly were not. The class climate suddenly changed from being conducive to learning to one of havoc, that's threatening the physical safety of my other students. My students had become irresponsible by acting irresponsibly. Out of nowhere, a group of students began laughing out loud, pointing at Sandy. I could hear students making unkind remarks: "She's stinking up the room." "Looks like she slept in her clothes." I didn't catch the students making the rude comments right away, but by the time I had, Sandy was up and standing in front of one of her tormentors. Her face showed astonishment as she stared speechless at her tormentors. Sudden anger lit up her eyes, and she became a boiling fury ready to erupt.

I rushed over, gently placed my hand on Sandy's shoulder, and told her to take her seat, promising to take care of the problem. Sandy was so angry that her hands trembled and her face flushed. I gently reached for her frail, trembling hands and placed them in mine. Her faced relaxed, her hands became still, and a gentle smile crossed her lips. The pressure of time intervened. I felt frustrated because I hadn't done a closing activity and the student homework assignment had not been assigned. I had lost control of "classroom management." When the dismissal bell rang and I dismissed the class, the other students departed, but Sandy just sat. Realizing that my fourth period class was waiting to enter, I approached Sandy and tried to calm her hurting heart. The belittling words of one student toward another can crush any spirit. Sandy later confided that she was homeless. That jolted me.

I realized much later that I had failed to handle the problem quickly enough. To minimize interruptions such as the one above, I should have allowed the students to continue in their engagement activity; this would have freed me to immediately handle the ensuing problem and the students involved. Management has a lot to do with everything.

4. HANDLE IT!

"The true worth of a man is not to be found in man himself, but in the colours and textures that come alive in others."

— *Albert Schweitzer*

"My teacher says I'm an underachiever, but I
think she's an overexpecter."

his parents were relieved. Until one day his mother discovered that I had dangled a carrot in front of Anthony. Now we'll see who buys the fast red car. But, here again, what do teachers want students to do? I would soon come to realize the pitfalls and the positive aspects of disciplining with rewards. Motivating my students to do their assignments was a big concern for me. My students knew and were reminded of my high expectations, and we worked diligently to complete assignments. *Oops! Is that what education is all about? Motivating students to complete assignments?* Remember, I was still in the discovery years. Actually, I recently discovered the truth about "motivation."

There are telltale signs of unmotivated students: a lack of a significantly high percentage of students achieving at or above the satisfactory level; a lack of student participation or a drop in student interest in the subject matter. On the other hand, I am reminded of an eighth-grade student who was the exception, but whom I didn't reward. Shawn approached each lesson with so much enthusiasm I just wished all of my students were like him. Sometimes, Shawn would smile and start right in on an assignment. Frankly, he was a delight compared to the other students. Shawn wasn't extremely smart, so he did not strike up any exceptional or exciting conversations. He had an air of confidence about him that reeked of success, so it was easy to give him praise. To create diversified learning, I provided Shawn with thought-provoking activities and hands-on projects. His grades and level of motivation soared! Shawn was concerned with his grades, but not the learning process. As a result, he often didn't do well on tests.

Oh, if only I had more students like Shawn. Frankly, Shawn did not need to have praise, carrots, or anything else dangled in front of him; he had already internalized success and failure. Marvin Marshall (2002) believes that rewards are great for acknowledging successful work, congratulating students, or demonstrating appreciation. Listen. There are two types of motivation: extrinsic and intrinsic. They are diametrically opposed (McKinney, 2009). When students are motivated by being rewarded for completing an assignment or getting a good grade, teachers frequently give them extra points, goodies, or playtime, rather like dangling a carrot in front of carnivorous students. But have they learned from the lesson or instruction? Intrinsic motivation is quite different: a love of learning or acquiring knowledge with the understanding that it is necessary, resulting in positive self-confidence.

This is the level at which teachers really want their students to be. Dangling a carrot doesn't encourage a student to think at the intrinsic level. So, what are strategies I could have used with Shawn?

First, I needed to get to know Shawn—his habits, likes, dislikes, academic background, and learning style; his non-graded pretest tapped into these questions. However, I didn't take the time to discuss with Shawn what the test revealed. I had way too many students to do that.

Second, I could have had a conversation with Shawn about the importance and long-term gain of really learning from the lessons instead of simply completing an assignment for the sake of getting a credit. I needed to help Shawn go from learning "helplessness" (McKinney, 2009), to learning that would build upon his attitude of being a responsible, self-confident learner.

Finally, after working through the first two steps, I could have provided Shawn with more learning activities that are engaging to students, such as scaffolding (where a more knowledgeable person provides support for the learner), creative activities, and hands-on projects with other students.

Darrell, on the other hand, was disruptive. I do believe he intended to annoy me with his misbehavior. Dangling carrots or any other incentives or rewards could not charm this kid into doing the right thing. Darrell's situation was just the opposite of Shawn's; his behavior was counterproductive; thus, I was challenged to making certain that a reward was not being given for counterproductive behavior, as that would have made the reward itself counterproductive.

I can see him now. Darrell's tall, slender, black-clad figure towered over the other students by a full three feet or more. The minute he hit the door, he started trouble. Darrell would come in, tough but extremely nonchalant, look at the daily organized language (DOL) or daily organized writing (DOW) or Essential Question (EQ), and deliberately decide not to do the work. He chose instead to chew paper and spit it at his neighbor. This, in turn, meant I would have to stop taking attendance and settle the argument. He had a stubborn arrogance in his face. This also meant disciplining Darrell. Talking was out of the question, but moving him outside the learning circle was not. You see, Darrell had restless energy and this caused problems. Darrell was always given two choices, never more than two. He could do the work or move to a corner of the room; his behavior often resulted in a call to his parents, which he did not like.

I recall the conversation. "Darrell, I have noticed you are the only one in class choosing not to do your English assignment, which was given out ten minutes ago. In fact, you have chosen to dawdle, kick the back of your neighbor's chair, and attempt to disturb your neighbors with unnecessary chatter." Students whined and complained of Darrell tapping a pen on the desk, letting out gas, and teasing working students. Darrell was the most talked about student among other teachers, and not in a positive way.

Slumped in his chair, he responded in a nonchalant tone, "I don't understand the assignment."

Almost pleadingly, I asked, "What is it you don't understand?"

"I don't know."

This was clearly a lie to cover up the fact that he did not want to do the assignment. At this juncture, he had two choices, the time-out wall and a parental call or referral to the principal. Darrell had not internalized his behavior and its consequences. Eventually, I removed him from the classroom and wrote a dean's referred. That led to a parent conference, where the dean reiterated the school policies and the consequences for violating rules. It was my hope that the dean's referral would be understood as punishment for Darrell's behavior, and that I would not see insubordinate misbehavior again. His cooperation resulted in decent grades, and helped to maintain an environment conducive to learning. However, in the weeks that followed the referral, Darrell eventually began to fall back into being insubordinate. I had to devise some other type of consequence for his behavior, or positive consequences for doing what was expected, because Darrell had not internalized the consequences for being insubordinate.

There are times when you have to give a student options and hope the student will make the most responsible choice. In this situation, Darrell needed guidelines and constant validation to change his behavior. He had plenty of opportunities to correct his behavior, but chose not to. It became important for me to identify the reasons behind Darrell's uncooperative and insubordinate spirit.

For two weeks, I documented Darrell's behavior. Toward the end of the quarter, the dean and I held another conference with Darrell. Darrell's behavior had not improved and I was convinced that he needed stronger discipline. I continued making parent contacts, sending notes home, requiring a signature, making calls home, and signing Darrell's daily planner. The notes never came back. His mother failed to understand that Darrell needed more motivation and remedial instruction. This meant I had to personalize Darrell's instruction. I provided him with some structure, made certain he understood what was expected of him, and ensured that he understood the lesson. Much of the time, he was provided with hands-on activities. I made sure he was given immediate feedback coupled with a simple reward for obtaining his goal. Darrell's mother fully understood my plight and offered her support. "Dr. Lindsey," said the mother, "you have our permission to do anything you see necessary to help our Darrell." Darrell gently smiled. The mother asked Darrell, "Do you want to graduate from high school?" Darrell responded, "Yes." Darrell's mother anxiously wanted me to see Darrell's hobby. He had an impressive collection of model trains he had built alongside model cars.

I was eager to discover ways that I could use Darrell's creativity to improve his academic performance. I let Darrell know he was a great person deep inside, but I needed to see positive behavior in class and further, I expected him to take responsibility for his learning.

Soon, Darrell eagerly entered class prepared to work. He had a new notebook, pens and pencils, plenty of paper, and a new attitude. You see, Darrell committed to doing his work first, and I promised him he could draw model cars when his work was completed. Darrell kept his commitment as I kept mine. In fact, Darrell's English work went up on the bulletin board and right next to it was a picture of his model car. According to Marvin Marshall in *Discipline Without Punishments or Rewards*, rewards are meaningful if the receiver of the reward is truly interested in the reward, and realizes that there are consequences for appropriate conduct. The reward Darrell received also served as a means of acknowledging that an appropriate behavior had been demonstrated. One would argue that Darrell should not have been given a reward for doing what was expected of him. I had hoped to teach Darrell values such as being responsible and respectful to others. Darrell was not bribed to act appropriately. He was strongly urged. Darrell understood that he could use his free time to work on his drawings only after completing all class work.

In the weeks following the teacher home visit, I observed Darrell closely, looking for signs of what he did well, his creativity. I noticed that Darrell was a great dreamer; this helped me to come up with creative writing projects. I tried to provide Darrell, and other students of like mind, with plenty of diverse lesson activities in order to encourage divergent thinking. Each time Darrell did something positive, I verbally rewarded him. Yep, I said rewarded—not in the most traditional way, giving him something tangible, but giving him an intrinsic reward in the form of explicit praise: "What a great story," "You've got the idea," "I knew you could write a really creative story." I guess my attitude about rewarding kids is based on my upbringing. My parents did not believe in giving us an allowance for doing simple tasks around the house, jobs we were expected to do because we lived there. But we received our allowance based on what we did over and above what was expected; sometimes, there was no monetary reward, but we got a pat on the back or words of value and appreciation. These intrinsic motivations were the best rewards ever, and I used the same technique with Darrell.

Darrell and other students earned both types of rewards, extrinsic and intrinsic. When they got a physical reward, students smiled and said, "Thanks." But when motivational words became their reward, their smiles widened, they stood tall, and said, "Thank you, Mrs. Lindsey," with joy in their voices.

First, the "carrot" strategy had to change. Darrell had other issues that likely contributed to his disregard for academic achievement. Thus I documented, on a daily basis, his behavior and academic performance: what he did well, his learning style, how he approached the learning task, how well he listened and interacted with other students, the level at which he performed a task, and his general attitude about the skill.

Second, by getting his parents involved, I was able to identify, detail, and discuss strategies that would encourage Darrell to become an intrinsic learner. What a job. To begin, I had Darrell write down the lesson objective for each assignment. On one side of a sheet of paper, he made lecture notes, and in the middle, he would write down the activity. On the other side, he would write what he'd done to complete the assignment. Just below the assignment, I had him summarize what he'd learned. Allowing Darrell a little extra time, monitoring his documentation, and assigning a partner to work with him really helped him on the road to recovering from being an undisciplined extrinsic learner. I began giving the class a variety of learning activities, some of which were choice-driven; they really liked that. It's cumbersome, but yields intrinsic motivation.

Third, I formed a learning community by involving Darrell's parents, his counselor, and the dean. At the end of each week, Darrell was responsible for completing a weekly progress report. That report had to be signed by his parents and returned to the counselor on Monday morning. I then followed up.

As teachers, we can't force students to become intrinsically motivated, but I think as instructors we are responsible for what students learn and how they learn it. We need to encourage and develop strategies that will help students become intrinsically motivated for a lifetime.

Reaching the Reluctant Learner: Before they Become Struggling Learners

Kindness begets kindness.

—Greek Proverb

The shuffling of student feet, lively chatter, hugging/slapping, and lots of laughter signaled the beginning of a new school year. I heard a young girl ask her friend, "Hey, Jessica, what happened with that guy you met at the party in the hood? Are y'all still dating?"

Her friend responded, "Girl he was something just for the summer."

The first day of a new school year had finally arrived. Nervous and anxious do not adequately describe what I was feeling minutes before meeting my first-period class, and it probably didn't describe how Jessica felt as she began her first day in a new school year. One of my colleagues made it his business to inform me of the types of students enrolled in our school: 35 percent white, 30 percent Hispanic, 25 percent black, and 10 percent other ethnic groups. Roughly 65 percent of our students were low achievers—at risk, unmotivated, and reluctant learners. Reluctant learners sit in every classroom. The challenge to all educators is putting the desire or fanning the flame back into reluctant learners. I found that reaching reluctant learners often become frustrated, extremely overwhelming, irritating, and sometimes disappointing and disheartening. It is likely that the reluctant learner is feeling some frustrations. Jessica was the one student in my sixth-period class I shall remember for a long time. Adopting new instructional strategies seems to be a never-ending process. Identifying and working with the reluctant learner means making effective instructional methods matter. I often think of reluctant learners as students who are experiencing difficulty keeping up with peers of the same age who are in a developmentally appropriate learning environment. I'm not speaking of a student who qualifies for special services, but a student who is not interested in education, not interested in what you are teaching, not interested in school at all. Deborah Burns (2008) further describes the reluctant learners as the student that is not engaged in learning activities or anything else that is connected to academics. Interestingly, this characteristic does not define how the learner reacts to situations outside the school environment. Learner reluctance isn't something that a student is born with; it is the lack of a cognitive function such as attribution—what the students attributes learning to. It is also a lack of motivation, whether extrinsic or intrinsic, and what value the student ascribes to motivation. Learner reluctance is a deficit of self-confidence—reluctant learners do not feel positive about their success, their skill attainment. The reluctant learner is one who has problems catching on to skills easily and quickly because of the way the instruction is presented, or is not able to perform within the allocated timeframe. Therefore, reluctant learners tend to perform poorly in most subject areas. Additionally, they often are not organized, because they are not able to sort out instructions. They don't immediately begin assignments and are likely to complain that they have too much work to do, and so they determine what work will be done and what won't. Finally, reluctant learners are daydreamers; they are not likely to be mentally engaged in your subject area. It is the reluctant learner who falls through the cracks. In the course of my years as a teacher, I used numerous strategies for reaching the reluctant learner. I do need to let you know that these strategies didn't work with all my reluctant students all of the time. There were students who just wouldn't do what they needed to do, despite my efforts.

Jessica was a low achiever by choice. Jessica would find a seat in the rear of the classroom preferably next to someone who she could converse with, slyly keep her head down, and hope that I wouldn't call on her to answer a question. I'm sure that Jessica wished that she could hide her poor academic performance in last year's Basic English class, and the repeated fear of failing this year. The challenge facing all teachers is knowing how to fan the flames back into reluctant learners, in other words developing strategies that are creative and will draw the interest of reluctant learners.

Jessica began experiencing problems in her home life toward the end of her sixth grade year, and as a seventh grader not much had changed at home. Jessica didn't get along with her mother. She wanted to run her own life while her mother wasn't going to allow that in her house. There were times when Jessica would tell her teachers that her mother was abusive, likely knowing that this would get the attention of her teachers and someone would call the authorities. Hoping that Jessica had put last year behind her and was ready to move forward with her education, I made it a point to develop a positive relationship with her. Jessica struggled with her classes and she struggled within. She had little enthusiasm for school. Once in a while she would bring a folder and a writing instrument but most of the time she was without both. Jessica's demeanor; her broad shoulders carried her burdens in her slothful walk. Jessica found it difficult to begin class assignments. She always complained that she didn't understand the assignment. However, when she did an assignment it was done well. So it wasn't that she couldn't do the assignments, she had so many outside distractions that she simply had trouble concentrating on school. To get away from her miserable, confused, and chaotic home life Jessica began to cut classes only to "hang out" with older boys from the neighboring high school. She eventually became a run-away.

When Jessica managed to come to school I treated her as a valued member of class, and often reminded her of our student academic commitments and behavioral expectations as she was a talker. I found myself deliberately going over to her seat and letting her know that I was glad she was in class. I began calling on her to solve English problems. Sometimes she was mentally in class other times she was only there physically. I eventually placed Jessica in a small group hoping this would help hew with getting class assignments completed, and that her group members would help her stay focused and engaged in the assignment. It was important for me to change learning activities. That was done by having students change activities every ten to fifteen minutes; that keeps the brain stimulated. I gave whole class instruction for ten to fifteen minutes, and thereafter students would move to different learning sites in the classroom. For example, computer site or zone, small group, reinforcement group—these students worked with me. Just ten minutes before the end of class students would return to their seats and we would do a oral review, paper/pencil assessment, and reflection. There were times when the assessment was oral, but the reflection was usually written in their journals. The small group wasn't good for Jessica. She used that time to engage in chatter about her outside lifestyle. She always had a captive audience as her group listened with anxious ears to the life of a seventh grade street girl. As Jessica would say "Hanging out is much more exciting than fixin' bad sentences." Easton (2008) call students like Jessica a "dis" kid. Meaning, she was disconnected, disinterested, disenchanted, disassociated, and disfranchised. Jessica would quickly affirm "School is not in my cards."

The time I spent working with Jessica became frustrating, irritating, and tiresome. Although I didn't see much academic growth, I did see a small percent of behavioral improvement. For example, the amount of times she used profanity in class decreased, and there was less talking and more listening. Jessica's attendance began to improve. I remember one day she decided to cut class. When most students cut class they hid out. Not Jessica. There were days when Jessica would sit on the railing across the street from my room, with her high school companions and bellow with her boisterous strong voice, "Hey Dr. Lindsey, do you miss me? I'm sorry I can't make class today." Or, "Hey Dr. Lindsey, I really like you and I know I'm missing out on some good English education." This went on for about a week. It got to the point where I anxiously waited to hear what message she had for me.

The school year passed and I never saw Jessica again, until she showed up at my church one Sunday. The one comment she made was, "Dr. Lindsey, I'd like to visit you in your home. Can I do that one day?" Well, sadly, she was placed in another home for run away children. At this writing Jessica is remains on the street somewhere.

There wasn't a "quick fix," nor a "blanket" warm enough, that any teacher could use in solving Jessica's complex problems. Why is it that educators are not able to reach the reluctant learners? What are the curriculum and instructional books leaving out that might grab the interest of reluctant learners? What are the educational psychological books leaving out? What are the early childhood texts leaving out?

Have educators considered the impact school culture has on students like Jessica? Easton (2008) suggests that by changing the school culture educators make learning more inhabitable for struggling learners, but what about the reluctant learner?

Caesar stood all of five inches short, very short for a ninth grader. His dark skin intensified his inky black hair and eyes. He was a very shy student. Caesar had limited reading skills but a *big* desire to learn how to read. He barely knew his vowel sounds; in fact, he wasn't able to identify vowels from consonants; and he had limited communication skills. There were days when I could not muster the strength to give Caesar the extra help he needed; he lacked the stimulation to go the extra mile to be an achiever. He was a struggling student, destined to become a reluctant student if I didn't come up with a strategy that would capture his mind and interest. I felt as though I had hit a roadblock and couldn't go much further. I decided to make some adaptations in my instruction strategies.

First, I needed to use creative instructional activities with Caesar, to let him know the relevance of reading and writing, and to give him confidence in the midst of failure. I began using stories on tape. According to Dr. Burns, in *Differentiation for Reluctant Learners* (2008), finding the hook stimulates students' interest. The hook needs to render success but be challenging. Instead of reading out loud in a small group, Caesar listened to stories on tape and responded to short, manageable comprehension questions; these included fill-in-the-blank and short-essay questions. I broke down the traditional lecture-type instruction by combining auditory and visual. I didn't give Caesar time to sit and chat, as he got involved immediately upon entering the class. I remembered to provide support throughout the class period. Thus, reinforcing Caesar's interest level, it became motivational, and increased his self-confidence. If I had known better, I would have looked for telltale signs of reluctance in Caesar, such as the passive way he began assignments. If I didn't direct Caesar, remind him of what he should be doing, or bring him back into the classroom, he would just sit.

Second, Caesar needed to taste hope, the sweetness that comes with any challenge. So, to create hope I helped him envision the successful outcome of a lesson—learning. I broke the assignment into small bite-sized pieces that would allow Caesar and other students to reach their maximum performance and see success at the end of the period. For example, instead of assigning an entire assignment from one chapter, I broke it up, or instead of assigning all thirty English sentences, I would assign the odd sentences and have my students write a descriptive paper as a group. I didn't begin adding the success formula until later in my teaching career: The three "r's"—redo + retake + revise = learning (Burns, 2008). I should have known to watch for Caesar being easily frustrated; I could have stepped up sooner. There were times when Caesar would start an assignment and stop after ten to fifteen minutes. This was a sign that he was inattentive because he was getting bored with the assignment (Burns, 2008).

This third instructional method was the most successful in improving Caesar's academic performance. I assigned him a buddy. As a reluctant learner, he was able to share notes, compare his answers to the assignment, and see the value of doing homework. At this point, parents were pulled into the learning. I elicited the help of parents, asking them to initial all homework. I was beginning to see success. Involving his parents provided Caesar with the additional emotional support needed from those closest to him, his family. There is nothing like building a student's self-efficacy. With Caesar it was cognitive and emotional self-efficacy that played a significant part in yielding success (Bandura, 1997).

Fourth, I put homework and daily work on different sides of the board. The assignments could be seen from any location in the classroom; I used vivid whiteboard markers, underlined, and placed borders around assignments. This helped Caesar sort out the directions. Caesar was able to work independently with the help of his Venn Diagrams. That was one of the goals that Caesar and I set: to be able to work independently. Another strategy that helped Caesar was the use of a storyboard. He retold stories in his own words, and then I let him color. This is a great activity for kinesthetic learners; it can easily replace the traditional paper-and-pencil assignment. Teaching a roomful of students can be laborious, but it is certainly more effective when we are able to identify students' learning styles. By identifying Caesar's learning style, I was able to adapt my method of instruction.

Fifth, there was time during the week when students had to do engagement exercises that required them to move around the room. I had to closely monitor the engagement lessons. It was important that

Caesar and other students had many opportunities in many different forms to practice a skill.

Finally, for assessment, I used weekly, formal, formative quizzes, unit tests, or software-based diagnostics. There were times when I allowed students to use some type of manipulative as a means of demonstrating their understanding and mastery of a skill they had been taught. Students were required to explain their work in writing. (*Effective Instructional Methods*, 2000).

One December day, out of the blue, Caesar said, "Thank you, Dr. Lindsey." Our smiles met as I asked him what he meant. Caesar responded, "You help me to read," and returned to his seat.

Naomi Remen, in *My Grandfather's Blessings* (2000), writes about making a difference. She says, "Sometimes when a life of service has taken us to the fringes of human experience, what we find there is so overwhelming that our hearts can break. One might think that compared to the size of the problem what we do means nothing, but this is simply not the case." She further gives an example:

Once in a medical meeting, someone asked another pediatrician, director of the adolescent clinic in one of New York City's inner city hospitals, how she could continue this work year after year when the kids she saw had so many special problems that nothing she did made a difference. "Why no," she replied with conviction. "With kids like these, everything I do makes a difference."

With Caesar, there were no physical rewards as I had used earlier in my career. Learning became something Caesar valued because he liked the feeling of being successful and he was able to see the relevance. Activating Caesar's desire to learn was the key to his progress (Sullo, 2007).

If a survey were taken on student motivation, an overwhelming number of teachers would agree that a large number of their students fall into one of the following categories: reluctant learners, unmotivated learner, or struggling learner. So why is America seeing so many students drop out of school, increased failures, and large numbers of students who are retained and underachieving? Researchers from the Carnegie Council (in *Adolescent Development*, 1996) suggest that there are many contributing factors, such as family and peer pressure, poor attendance, behavior problems, social and emotional problems, medical issues, and attitude. In addition, researchers found that parental attitudes, unsupportive parents, parent values, low academic skills of parents, low expectations from teachers, ineffective instructional methods, and failure of teachers to use components of an effective or appropriate instruction activity were significant determinants of disengagement. A final cause of underachievement is the lack of strong and sustained guidance from a caring adult. These are factors affecting students at an early age and continuing through high school. An ASCD Weblog (2008) cited comments regarding motivating the reluctant learner. Their comments are echoed across the country:

"We can motivate reluctant learners by personally getting to know them. It could be that they are unmotivated by the lack of concern." Wolk (2008) postulates that teachers need to provide relevant experiences for the reluctant learner. Those relevant experiences are important features of the learning process. The teachers below articulate their concerns with reaching reluctant learners.

Mary writes: "It is always a challenge finding ways to motivate the reluctant learner. Learning styles should be taken into consideration when working with reluctant learners. Differentiating an assignment can often be the key!"

According to Denise, "I have found that many of the students I work with are so burned out from testing preparation that they become extremely unmotivated. I have to push them to keep working hard at school My students set goals and do individual checks of their personal goals throughout the year. We all celebrate when a goal has been made and then the students set another goal. I feel that this teaches my students to stay motivated, both in school and in their personal lives."

Teachers who are successful in the classroom identify models for learning that reach underachievers—unmotivated, reluctant, and struggling learners. Even then, there remain students who are struggling, unmotivated-disinterested, or underachievers. Let's look further at models for reaching students that are at risk. The use of hands-on, high-interest activities and activities that challenge students to think are needed. For example, teachers might consider project-based learning. This approach allows students to demonstrate their learning by creating projects along with designated classmates. These might include posters, displays, plays, or performances, even the use of technology.

Teachers must provide students with meaningful, engaged learning

Reaching the Unmotivated Learner

Enthusiasm is the invisible source of energy that children find so attractive and contagious. You light the match, and they will carry the torch.

—Greg Henry Quinn

Like so many other teachers, I needed to know why I had students who just didn't have the desire to be achievers. In an average class of thirty to thirty-five students, I could calculate at least two students who would just sit in wonderland watching the class period race by, doodling or just not getting involved. They had no yearning to get involved in acquiring knowledge or put forth no effort in getting involved in the class activities. I began to ask myself what I was doing wrong. What else did I still need to do? After all, I'd implemented the strategies gained from those weekly staff meetings. Where was I going wrong? What was it I failed to understand about the unmotivated student? Why was I still not able to reach those seemingly unmotivated students? I needed help. Learners who were left out of the circle of learning began to be my central focus. It got to the point that I found it difficult to face the classes that had unmotivated students in them, until one day a colleague helped me to see the unmotivated learner through a new set of lenses.

"What do you teach?" asked a high school history teacher, as we chomped down on delicious finger foods at a district professional development meeting for teachers.

"Middle school," I said.

He responded, in a tone of awe and respect, "You teach middle school?"

"Yep," I said.

"God bless those middle school teachers. You have my admiration. Middle school students have got to be the worst kids on planet earth. They are noisy, unsettled socializers, rebellious, annoying, and not the least bit motivated to learn. In fact, they are bored and boring." Without taking a breath, he continued, "High school students, on the other hand, are more interesting, academically motivated, and more adult-like." I had taught high school for ages and I certainly didn't agree much with this guy.

I was most anxious to find out what district he was speaking of and asked sarcastically, "Is this a school located in a district in the United States?" Then, in a more patient and agreeable tone, I said, "I could not agree with you more. A middle school teacher has to be up to the challenge of teaching unmotivated, sometimes bored middle school students." I wanted this high school teacher to feel what it was like trying to reach the unreachable students like Josh, Jennifer, and Matt. I had hoped, for some reason, that he would have answers for reaching them because I didn't. I wasn't interested in spending time at a district meeting eating, reviewing old strategies, or listening to boring speakers tell teachers what we weren't doing right; after all, it's always a teacher's fault. But today I needed some grounded understanding of unmotivated students so that I would be able to apply new strategies for reaching them. So, excuse me, sir, while I tell you about three students who were consistently on my mind.

A teacher would need a sense of humor to teach students like Josh, who arrived at school with green hair, or Jennifer, who wore earrings larger than her ears, and decided, early in the seventh grade, that she didn't need an education. Besides, her only ambition was to be a strip teaser and race up and down a pole. This is the truth. Then there is Matt. Matt constantly challenged my level of tolerance with a cynical and devilish look in his eyes. Matt had a high absentee rate and felt that school was really boring. He didn't feel that his teachers challenged him and once stated, "My teachers don't know much."

Middle school can be a rebellious time, but it is a time of measurable academic, emotional, and social growth. Most middle schoolers enjoy reading, writing, talking, and thinking about subjects that affect them. Trying to reach students who don't seem to give a care about school or learning has been a problem for educators and educational researchers for years. I am speaking about students who appear to have lost interest in learning; their lack of motivation is easily recognizable. They are droopy, seem unmotivated, fail to respond to the learning process, and are physically sitting in a seat yet mentally absent. Can you imagine how frustrating this has to be for teachers? It never ceased to amaze me to watch elementary students gaily engaged in the classroom and happily motivated to get to school. They are curious and soak up the idea of exploring. I'm talking about the simplest things, like catching a frog. Then when these same students hit middle school, that motivation, enthusiasm, curiosity evaporates. There are usually students who do not respond to teaching, no matter what strategies you use. This was the case with Matt.

Matt was stocky built, about six foot five, with thick black hair, and two-inch fingernails. He had a snotty attitude, a cold demeanor, and a macabre, hidden personality about him. I didn't trust him. It was not unusual for Matt to make rude, condescending comments about me or about the learning activity. This is a student that was not a favorite with any of his teachers. Whenever we passed, he would snarl as though he were some wild animal. There were times when I used a technique called mobile roaming, quietly positioning myself in a student's space, even giving that student "the look." This usually would get students back on task or cause them to check their behavior. But this technique didn't always work with Matt.

In a defensive, impatient, and anxious gesture, I folded my arms across my chest. It seemed as though the morning announcements would never end. Finally, it was time to begin my reading workshop lesson. I had previously read aloud a portion of *Julie of the Wolves*, as reading aloud nurtured me as well as my students and set the tone for our class workshop. I instructed the students to make notes of thoughts and questions as I read and then work in their groups after I finished. They found their way to desks arranged in five communities. I told one group to discuss words that described the characters' personalities; I told another group to identify the story's themes by making general statements. While the larger groups were meeting, I chose to work with struggling readers in two small groups.

While walking around the room, I noticed that Matt was not on task; he was drawing. I heard him say, "This is so juvenile. I don't wanna do this." This was how Matt usually acted in class. I reiterated the class expectations, offered consequences, reviewed the group's mission and time line, and told them what to do upon completion. Finally, I said firmly, "This is your book, Matt." Matt gave me an arrogant grin, shook his head, and said, "Oh no, Mrs. Lindsey, I don't read books." I persisted. "This book is yours. You need to begin working on your group's assignment and I don't want to see you drawing." Shrugging, picking up his book, and walking away, Matt mumbled under his breath obscenities that he thought would offend me. For certain, Matt had the attention of his peers, and he did not want to look bad in front of them. Engagement of middle school and high school students is highly influenced by peers. Neither of these groups of learners wants to fail at anything; to fail carries negative perceptions.

A few days later, I received an urgent message in my mailbox. Matt's father had requested a teacher conference with me right away. With some reluctance and a certain amount of dread, I passed the message on to the counselor's secretary who called Matt's parents to schedule a parent conference.

Matt's parents were surprised to learn of his consistently inappropriate attitude in three of his classes. Matt had more behavioral problems in his reading class. "We understand Matt has an attitude problem with you because he simply doesn't like you." Matt failed to understand that his attitude affected his academic performance. "We'd like to know what you've done to our son," said his mother. "The other day he walked in, complaining as usual, with a book. He said, 'Mom, you've got to read the last chapter of this book to me and I have to write down five questions from the chapter.'"

I was surprised that Matt had bothered with the assignment at all. We decided that Matt would have to do all assignments and we would challenge him to be a group leader or peer helper. Matt needed to realize that learning is an intensely personal experience in order to have a lasting effect. I decided to recognize Matt's positive behavior and work as many times as possible.

There is nothing like a student with a negative attitude. If a teacher had to choose between a student with poor academic performance and one with good academic performance but a negative attitude, it would be difficult to decide which one would be the worse. I have a problem with students who have bad attitudes, period. When I tell—not ask—a student to do something, I expect that student to comply.

Matt had a problem in this area. I want students to move when I tell them to, not when they're ready, sulking and complaining. That's the bottom line. Matt refused to toe the line. So, I came up with a plan that would address his attitude problem and his smart mouth. I needed to be clear with Matt's problem. He didn't have a behavior problem Matt had a smart-aleck mouth.

According to an article by McCombs, B. L. & Pope, J. E. (1994), motivation is a word used often, but often misunderstood. "Lack of motivation" may mean that students are bored, lazy, or uninterested. The causes of these types of behavior are multidimensional; they range from how a student perceives a particular outcome, to how a student measures his or her self-worth based on a teacher's feedback, to the student's assigned expectations for attaining some level of performance and the value the student places on that performance. Therefore, teachers need to take into account a student's expectations and values for performing some identified task (McGrew and Evans, 2004). Keep in mind that expectations and values may be linked to the student's family's cultural values. A student's self-efficacy is defined by how the student plans to implement a course of action for obtaining some level of performance (Schunk, 2001). The unmotivated student "lack[s] … a student's willingness, need, desire and compulsion to participate in, and be successful in, the learning process" (Bomia, 1997). With all that has been defined, what can a teacher do to reach an unmotivated student? Consider that lack of motivation may not cause learning deficits, but students will likely not attain specific academic performance outcomes because of a lack of neurodevelopment.

Let's go back to the story of Matt. I told Matt it would be necessary to have a parent-teacher conference about his attitude problem in reading class. The conference was arranged. We talked to Matt about his attitude, citing examples where necessary. Matt agreed that the accounts were accurate. So, we developed a plan. I decided to observe Matt's interaction with others, evaluate his work in terms of project completion, homework, participation with peers when engaging in group work, and his state of mind when attending to a task.

First, Matt and his parents needed to understand that when Matt was told to do something he was to do it right then, not when he was ready. His parents indicated that Matt only moved when he was ready at home, also. This did not surprise me. According to Strong et al.

(1995), when trying to reach unmotivated students a teacher must make certain that the student understands learning expectations for performance and behavior; teachers must be firm and consistent when managing behavior and the learning environment.

Second, Matt had to do his work carefully and completely. Matt did his work the way he wanted to. I explained the long-term effects of doing it "his" way. I pointed out that it would be dangerous to carry this attitude into high school or into a job situation. Research indicates that it is imperative that teachers promote mastery of a skill. Matt had to complete the assignment based upon specific criteria; he was given two opportunities to redo the assignment, with the help of a rubric.

Third, Matt had to speak respectfully to his peers and to me at all times. I indicated that Matt would need to think about what he wanted to say before saying it. He was to keep all negative, impolite comments to himself. I gave him an example of the kinds of unkind comments he made, and followed it up with comments that were more appropriate. On one particular day, I found it necessary to clearly articulate my expectations for Matt's behavior. "Matt, today I told you to put your art work away, turn to page eighty-eight in your literature book, and listen for details about the story. Instead, you made a smart-aleck comment when you said, 'This is a stupid lesson.' Your attitude was out of line with what you were told to do." Working to build a positive relationship with students is critical (McCombs and Pope, 1994). His parents agreed that he had an attitude problem at home and that he was stubborn. "He always wants his way." Again, I wasn't surprised. This was going to be a major undertaking.

Finally, to check that Matt understood what was expected of him, a written contract was hand-delivered to the counselor and to his parents in a follow-up parent conference. A goal accomplishment, a timeline for academic improvement, and the consequences for not meeting our expectations were spelled out. As Matt progressed through his program, his attitude was kept in close check by all of his teachers; this was necessary to establish consistency. There was another parent-teacher conference where we all assessed his academic performance and the improvement in his attitude.

In the end, Matt barely made it through the first semester, he was eventually transferred into another reading class, and his parents ended up putting him into an outside counseling program. Matt completed seventh grade, not without problems. His teachers continued to follow the expectations I'd set. He made it to eighth grade. I later learned that Matt's attitude toward authority figures improved and would continue to improve.

The encounter with Matt created a deep concern for not only working with specific discipline problems, but, more importantly, understanding the student him/herself, and identifying useful strategies that will put the student on a track for academic success. I realized that all learning experiences are not interesting, fun, personally meaningful, or seemingly relevant to middle school students. In most cases, students who are not motivated see the academic nature of school as boring, tedious, meaningless, and irrelevant. I came to the conclusion that middle school students, and maybe high school students, learned best when I offered choices in the learning activities. The idea of offering choices to students, those who did not appear to be intrinsically motivated, seemed overwhelming. I offered Matt an alternative activity; one that was enriching, meaningful, and where he felt more in control. I had hoped this strategy would allow Matt to experience some measure of academic success. To access Matt's need for motivation and increase his level of interest, I developed activities wherein Matt was able to use his art skill as a part of the reading lesson.

Multiple activities allow for inductive teaching to take place. The activities should address diverse learning paradigms that tap into diverse learning types and skills. They must be carefully planned to meet district and state benchmark guidelines and strict mandates on what skills students need in preparation for student assessments. Offering choices moved my level of thinking about motivating unmotivated students to another dimension. Developing written lessons that allow for student creativity, self-expression, enjoyment, and improved academic performance is what leads to successful academic performance for the unmotivated learner.

5. THE VISITOR

"Things turn out best for the people who make the best of the way things turn out."

— *John Wooden*

"Your son stopped passing notes to his friends in class. Now he's text messaging them."

Communicating with Parents: When Parents Are from Saturn and Teachers Are from Venus

Some do the sowing, others the reaping.

—*Italian Proverb*

Teachers are often critical of parents, and parents are often critical of us. We express a strong desire for more parent participation; however, when parents step in, teachers tend to complain that they are bothersome. What's a parent to do? Or what's a teacher to do? I have had discussions with my colleagues over the years, and the verdict is still out about who is the worst. One teacher expressed her concern in the following way: "Many of the parents don't really care because they are mostly concerned about putting food on the table. I like working in Title One schools because parents don't participate, and I don't want to bother with them." Another colleague stated, "I'm tired of taking the role of parent, counselor, and teacher. These aren't my kids, I didn't have one of them. Therefore, parents need to step up to the plate and take full responsibility for their son/daughter's education."

Finally, a seasoned teacher spoke: "I agree that parents need to be more involved in the educational process, but oftentimes they get in the way. On one hand, I've seen parents try to teach a skill at home differently from the way I teach it. Then there are the parents who don't do what they can—check homework, practice spelling words, practice simple multiplication tables." The single basic element that binds parent involvement across the grades is grades; as far as parents are concerned, their son's or daughter's grade is paramount, not what they have learned. Those parents who are actively involved constantly and unwittingly undermine the work teachers are doing in the classroom. For example, many parents express an interest in their son/daughter's academic success but don't actively participate, they don't take the initiative to contact teachers, and forget to come to open house after students leave elementary school. Further, they want their son/daughter to get good grades, but fail to focus on "what is learned." Then there's the issue of discipline. They want you to be the disciplinarian, having the attitude that "you have them most of the day; don't call me. I don't know what to do with them." No wonder students manipulate their parents into believing that teachers are the bad guys. But there are times when teachers find themselves being critical of parents. The real concern is finding a break-even point at which parents and teachers can get along.

However, there are potential hindrances to parental involvement: parents may overreact to students' performance, they may have different expectations from that of the teacher, the teacher may find it difficult to build rapport with a parent, and there may be poor communication between parents and the teacher. There was a point in my teaching career when I wished there was no parental involvement.

Rudyard Kipling wrote, "We have forty million reasons for failure, but not a single excuse." I only wish Kipling were around to hear Evan's story.

Evan was a middle-school student trapped by his parents' poor judgment and his desire to be a successful student. Evan was in my accelerated reading class. He was smaller than the average seventh-grader; he actually looked like a fifth- or sixth-grader. He was short, with a small-boned frame. Evan had black, silky, straight hair; and every now and then, he would mousse it up. He was easy to spot in a crowded middle school corridor as he confidently pulled his roller bag daily. According to Evan's classmates, he was a loner.

Highly qualified teachers value and respect the role of parents' involvement in their children's education; if teachers are at the center of the education process, parents are the outer layer of the process that supports teachers. Even though parents are the primary education agency, teachers are often more knowledgeable about the learning process. Thus, they help parents understand the school's role in helping their children become higher achievers—responsible, literate, and articulate young men and women who will be able to make important contributions to our society. Teachers know how to use different assessment tools in determining student learning that allow teachers to plan appropriate instruction and determine student progress. With that in place, teachers share assessment results and help parents understand the teacher's role in helping their son/daughter become more knowledgeable.

Teachers establish two-way communication between parents and the school. They seek information from parents about their sons' and daughters' strengths, interests, study habits, and learning goals. As Evan's teacher, I earnestly tried to work closely with his parents in his best interest.

Evan was creative, polite, eager to learn, and a regular contributor in class discussions. However, Evan's comprehension was below grade level. He would often not follow directions for his assignments, and he seldom completed in-class assignments. He worked at a slow pace, yet he carried himself with a strong air of quiet self-assurance and did not let his poor performance intimidate him. He was so atypical. Most adolescents are full of energy, but Evan usually showed signs of fatigue in his eyes and was listless in class. Adolescents want to be independent from their families, but Evan allowed his parents to take the dominant role in his school. They chose his classes.

"Evan, have you completed your short-response paragraph? We've been on this five minutes now." Often I would defer further class discussions in order to include Evan. I did what I knew to do. First, as was my custom, I established consistently fair yet high learning expectations, and I shared these expectations with Evan's parents. I adjusted the expectations as needed. I strongly believe that establishing high expectations encourages students to reach beyond mediocre, and increases the likelihood that they will do better than they usually do.

Evan's parents had knowledge of his failing grade early in the semester, but chose not to respond until the end of the semester. I encouraged them to set high but reasonable academic expectations. I also suggested they place Evan on a daily progress-report program, and spend time with him daily, discussing his progress report: citizenship, grades, and work habits.

My administrator and I let his parents know the importance their attitude to Evan's grades, as well as the necessity of working together for the good of Evan. They both agreed. I recapped the agreement and I sent them a written copy of the contract agreement. However, after about three months, the relationship tumbled, as did Evan's grades.

When you have been in the teaching field for a long time, these sorts of setbacks occur frequently. As teachers, we give teaching our best. All of us attempt to communicate with parents with care. But there are times when, despite our efforts, we are fighting a losing battle.

Evan's parents refused to accept his "D" grade. We had numerous parent-teacher conferences during which I had to defend Evan's grades. I was always armed and ready for the battle; I was not afraid. With each conference, Evan's father became progressively more agitated. He yelled and began making personal attacks, including that I failed to motivate his son. Once he threatened to bring a lawsuit against me and take me to the media. I knew that oftentimes, the expectations of parents and teachers differ, so I tried to determine their expectations and align them with the results of Evan's assessment results. His parents refused to accept his assessment scores. I knew this might pose a problem.

Evan had strict instructions from his parents: He was not to do any class work in reading and he was to accept an "F" as his grade— all because his parents did not like me. To prevent a failing mark, the counselor offered to move Evan to another reading class. Evan's parents refused. They chose to humiliate their son and deny him the opportunity to achieve success in a critical life skill. I was devastated by this irresponsible parent decision. I realized that Evan's parents had views of learning and instruction that differed from mine. Always respectful of their perspective, I suggested a workable solution that I suggested a workable solution that would continue aligning district standards to instruction, learner outcomes, activities, and student assessments.

Throughout the school year, I continued communicating with Evan's parents: writing messages in his journal and making certain one of the parents signed it, keeping a log of telephone calls and details of the call, and placing him on a weekly progress report program. In addition, I informed his parents of upcoming special projects and events, as well as special units. Evan remained in my accelerated reading class to the end. His determination to see things through is a perfect example of what it takes to be a responsible learner. I continued to give him opportunities to succeed, but he eventually closed down, refusing to turn in any class work. Evan went on to the ninth grade, and I'll never know if I strengthened his reading comprehension and organization skills. I suppose the real test will come when he gets to the eleventh grade and takes the high school proficiency exam.

I think of Evan often and wonder if there was something else I could have done for him. Perhaps his parents should have been referred for parent counseling. Evan's situation reinforced the importance of developing a respectful working relationship among parents, teacher, and student. It is important to take all the necessary steps to gain influence with parents and establish your seriousness with them. The scenario below somewhat illustrates Evan's story.

Mr. Clam: "Come in, Mr. And Mrs. Neddle, I've been expecting you."

Mr. And Mrs. Neddle: "We understand there is a problem with our son's grade in your English class. Jed has never had any grade problems before this."

Mr. Clam: "Well, that's not at all true. I'm holding his grade report for all of his classes. It appears that Jed has a D in math, a D in science, another D in explorations class, and a D in P.E.

Mrs. Neddle: "What's wrong with Ds? I graduated from high school with Ds and I don't do so bad in life."

Mr. Clam: "Is that all you want for Jed?" Are you willing for Jed to just sit in a class and earn a D? I was hoping that we could come up with a working plan before his grade began to drop.

Mr. Neddle: "By the way, what is his grade in your English class?"

Mr. Clam: "He has a D. I was just trying to shake you out of your

When Someone Else
Is Standing In Your Shoes

Problems are the cutting edge that distinguishes between success and failure.
Problems create our courage and wisdom.

—*M. Scott Peck*

Stepping into the shoes of another teacher, whether for the first time or as a regular substitute, can be absolutely scary. Substitute teachers face very challenging unique, unknown, and often unprepared-for challenges. The challenges face substitutes in all grades, from elementary school to high school. They are usually the same. Those challenges come with teaching different classes each day. Finding success as a substitute teacher isn't always easy, but it is possible. Successful substituting means the substitute and the teacher must prepare themselves. A teacher who takes the time to leave substitute lesson plans is a teacher who cares when someone else is wearing his or her shoes. Let's take a look at a most memorable experience I had as a substitute teacher. I had promised myself that I was never going to be a substitute teacher, but I found substituting a way of keeping my teaching skills charged while Pursuing my PhD.

My heart always goes out to subs. They have to endure unpredictable classrooms that can be like jungles. Substitutes often walk into classrooms filled with chaos and problem students.

I remember my first experience with substitute teaching. The ringing telephone broke my deep sleep around 7:00 AM Would I take an assignment at an elementary school in a lower-income area of the city? My head shook in hesitation, but my voice said, "Sure." Knowing the principal played a big part in my decision. I was assigned to a kindergarten class for three days. There were to have been two substitutes in the class, but the other substitute backed out. Now I know why. I figured the classroom aide and I could handle kindergartners. What should have been a teachable three days turned out to be a horrible experience waiting to be corrected.

I carefully read the scant substitute lesson plans: Rules and routine academic plans for reading, math, and language for the three days. The regular teacher left plans for the children to play games, do a lesson at the computer center, and then play some more, and had the nerve to end with, "Oh yes, have a good day." I guess she figured the aide would fill in the other important and necessary information.

The first day, I expected to greet the students in their line. I was wrong. After the first bell, signaling them to line up, the students were still running around. The classroom aide whispered as she stood next to me, "They don't listen. They should be lined up." Instead, the aide and I found ourselves yelling for the students to get in line; at one point, the aide began chasing students down. I had always heard that kindergarten kids want to please, sit still, do their work, and love their teachers. Much to my surprise, these little bodies were far from being cooperative. Let me get into my substitute story.

The aide and I had to physically corral the students into a line. I was no fool; this was where I needed to put my foot down. They were not exactly docile beneath their innocent kindergarten appearance. There lurked the possibility for big-time disaster, and I would be ready.

When I see the word "kindergarten" and its spelling, I immediately recognize the words "kind" and "tender"—words associated with babies, little ones, children not capable of terrorizing a teacher or the classroom. This class gave the word "kindergarten" a new meaning.

After entering the room, I decided to wait and get a feeling for what kinds of students I would be teaching. The first half hour was spent reading in groups; the aide had one group, and I had another. Meanwhile, there were other students working on a reading assignment at their desks. Suddenly, I watched in horror something I didn't expect. I stood bristling as students climbed under the tables, ran around the room, and threw crayons. Three of them were stomping on top of the desks while four or five were chalking up the chalkboard. There were students chasing one another around the room; two others had taken paint, left out by the regular teacher, and smeared it on the easels. Enough! Enough! Enough! I wondered what advice Harry Wong, educator, author on classroom management and student achievement would give me for this situation. I managed to stop the commotion and get on with the first day. I knew that the next two days had to be totally different. I needed a plan.

I quieted the students down and began reading my rules. I dared them to move, and not a student did. I made them surrender their misbehaviors. I substituted my plans for their regular teacher's lesson plans. I had to get and keep control. The aide and I quickly devised group activities, quiet time, and no playtime. Playtime was now something the students had to earn back. Day one passed with no further classroom upheavals and no student rebellions.

When the morning bell rang on day two, every student lined up without hesitation. There they remained until I appeared to retrieve them. With my arms folded, I watched as the students quietly entered class and stood next to their chairs, where they waited for further instruction. I cheerfully told the students how pleased I was with the way they lined up and entered class. The students cheered. I wanted to relax the students, so I proceeded to do the weather, review the alphabet, and count numbers up to fifty.

Language time was fun. I decided to read the students a story. Little eyes danced as I acted out different parts of the story. The students sat anxiously, wondering how the story would conclude. Day two ended on a high note. Each student bade me good-bye and skipped merrily out the door.

My last day, number three, was somewhat sad. The students and I had bonded. The faces of these kindergartners were eager, trusting, and filled with wonderment. I had conquered the problem in this classroom—lack of classroom management. It no longer would be a jungle but would be a classroom filled with loving, energetic, excited, motivated, enthusiastic, cheerful little beavers. On day three, they were just like little angels marching to every beat. I was pleased. For three days, I had created colorful classroom posters, learning centers, private reading centers, hands-on math and science, and easy but exciting listening and writing centers. I even came up with a king and queen for the day; I had to include his or her escorts so every student would eventually be acknowledged.

This three-day job was well worth my time. These kindergarteners had learned a big lesson in being responsible students. The aide said, "This is the first time in my two years of being in this class that I have been at peace. I wish you could take this class for the rest of the year."

I have heard horror stories like the one following from other substitutes. One such teacher accepted a substitute position with a local inner-city high school. "These students were the worst I've ever taught. I recall a couple of students making rude comments—'You're nothing but a substitute, you can't teacher us anything.' They called me names, 'You're a b____,' 'stupid substitute.'" She found that middle school as well as high school students tend to be disrespectful, hostile, loud, and obnoxious and often think that when there's a substitute, it's a time to party. To solve the discipline problems, the substitute sent misbehaving students to neighboring teachers, often called using the APOS system. She tried calling the security officer and even the principal, both of which only helped for a short while. "Once security and the principal left the room, the students started where they left off. You don't know how this makes a substitute feel. I left notes for the teacher and never received any gratitude."

Teachers, let's take a look at a few steps you can incorporate that will help substitutes experience a successful day. Please remember that a substitute lesson plan differs from a lesson plan a teacher would write for the normal day. Based on what substitutes have shared with me, many classroom teachers leave lesson plans that are written for the regular classroom teacher.

First, leave lessons that are written in short, simple form. Don't make them wordy, as though you are writing lesson plans for your administrator. Keep them simple. Note the page number(s), or worksheet, and additional materials that will make the lesson. If the substitute needs to give special instruction, then certainly tell him or her how. For example, if students are to take notes, let the sub know that. By all means, leave an example of what the students' work should look like.

Second, make certain your lesson plans list the bell schedule from the start of the first class to the end of the day, and all in-between activities, if you are elementary. I would also include a map of the school and emergency procedures, with expectations and major policies attached. For example, when I taught middle and high school, I wouldn't give bathroom passes. Include student activities where students work in groups or circles; actually, I try to avoid such learning activities. If students move to other classrooms for tutoring, do leave a list of names for the substitute.

Third, I always let the substitute know what to do with student work, whether it's completed or not. Do they place it in a particular box? Do they complete the assignment as homework? Do they keep it and turn it in upon your return? There were times when I would give more work than necessary, but I always sorted it out for my substitute. For example, all necessary work was noted as required and had a note attached. The extra credit work was labeled as extra credit, and I let the sub know that it was to be completed after the required work. Incidentally, I would always give work that had already been thoroughly taught, not anything new.

Another thing subs want to see is your duty schedule. If you have duty such as hall, bus, or crossing guard on the day you have a substitute, let the sub know where and when.

I can't tell you how important a seating chart is. There are so many teachers who don't have one, but when you have a substitute you need to create one. The seating chart not only helps in identifying students, but it lets the sub know who is in whose seat, and helps identify disruptive students. That's a real secret to helping the sub manage the class and is an excellent tool for managing discipline.

Making a folder or sub toolkit is helpful for placing all substitute directions. I suggest you make a substitute form and fill in the particulars when you need a sub. For example, substitute date, beginning-of-class procedures, class(es), assignment (pages/worksheet), end-of-class procedures (what to do with student work), private eyes (helpers), list of potential behavioral problems, and end notes (substitute notes). I also name support teachers who are willing to accept behavioral problems, along with their room numbers. By all means, tell the sub where students with special needs should go. Always leave referral slips for disruptive students. My sub always appreciated my leaving a one-page substitute teacher's report form, where the substitute leaves notes for each class. This is a detailed description of any problems or concerns.

Finally, identify two to three students from your class(es) who can be "private eyes." They are a helpful resource to substitutes; they can help pass out papers, collect papers, and note who disrupters are.

The substitute's goal is to continue the learning process without interrupting the normal flow of the learning environment. They will love you.

6. EXHALE

"*I have fought a good fight. I have finished the race, I have kept the faith.*"

— *2 Timothy 4.7*

"Uh-oh, teacher burnout!"

The Meeting Place:
The Teachers' Lounge

A single conversation with a wise person is better than ten years of study.

—*Chinese Proverb*

The places where individuals meet on a regular basis are sacred and special. For teachers, the teachers' lounge is such a place. The teachers' lounge is a place where colleagues offer one another support and encouragement, where teachers find solitude and are able to catch their breath. It is a place where ideas are exchanged and decisions are made over coffee and doughnuts. It is the place where teachers can regain strength to face the next class, the next day. It is the place where we voice our concerns; with the unwritten agreement that "what happens or is said in the lounge … stays in the lounge."

The teachers' lounge is probably the most valued place in the entire school. This is the "spot" where almost anything can happen. I have seen lounges that rock with laughter and fun, and lounges that are dull, drab, and simply lifeless. The lounge can be a place where teachers come for therapy; it's cheaper than sitting on a psychiatrist's couch to the tune of two hundred dollars an hour.

I have been in lounges where the conversation is strictly gossip—in other words, they talk about other colleagues, especially novice teachers; they talk about retirement, they talk about the administrators. (Do they have enough administrative experience, especially when it comes to telling veteran teachers what to do?) I've been in lounges where there is general conversation: the weather, kids, the help circle, food, vacation destinations, teacher salaries (a big one in all lounges); they remind each other of pay day. Then there is talk of family (Does someone have advice on how to get the twenty-five-year-old out of the house? Teachers are always trying to give advice); new building policies; the superintendent; and much more.

I have seen lounges that are cheerfully, colorfully decorated. I've seen lounges that are colorless—the paint was a dead color. I often wondered if the lounge tells us something about the staff personality in the building. I have seen all types of teachers come into the teachers' lounge.

There are teachers who come in who are veterans in the system. These are folks that have been around fifteen or more years. They know it all, or they think they do. You can't tell them too much they don't already know. They are funny. Once I overheard a group of veteran teachers bad mouthing a novice teacher. It appears that the new person on the block had big ideas for moving the school ahead of where they were, and that didn't sit well with the veterans, especially after hearing that the novice teacher was favored by the principal. Ouch! That hurts a veteran teacher's status.

Then there are folks who want suggestions on how to handle students' behavioral problems. There are teachers who just want to complain about anything that strikes their fancy, most likely something that is on the front page of the daily newspaper. Finally, there are teachers who really pour out their hearts, they need answers to more serious concerns: administration problems, poor evaluation—what do I do? Teacher surplus—what happens next? "I'm getting a divorce, how much do I take?"

I once had a colleague who had strong beliefs about the teachers' lounge. "I usually stay out of the teachers' lounge because you hear so much conversation about what the students can't do and how dumb they are. It got to the point where I would quickly change the subject. The teachers would look at me as if to say, 'You don't have student problems? Do you have special privileges with the dean?' One said, 'I guess after a while that negative conversation gets to you.'"

Often, when something or someone ails us, we look for places to dump the pain. Teachers carry around a lot of baggage from other people's children. The teachers' lounge seems to be the burial ground or morgue for getting rid of whatever bothers them.

Wherever these places may be, it reminds us that we are human beings standing in need of a campground, clinic, morgue, or meeting place. It may be a place where teachers can transform their pain into healing.

Teachers, like other humans, need a place to refuel. The meeting place can be a perfect place where teachers can pour out their heartaches and find consoling listeners. The teachers' lounge isn't all bad.

Finding Inner Healing

Muster your wits; stand in your own defence;
Or hide your heads like cowards, and fly hence.

— *William Shakespeare*

Most of us have suffered from some type of trauma. Whether it stems from something that has happened in the family or on the job, whether it relates to illness, death, or more worldly loss, a trauma is a trauma. People who are afflicted by trauma are in need of healing. Inner healing occurs when we experience relief and release from the hurt that has come into our lives, those hurts that cripple us or keep us down. There are plenty of teachers out there who have experienced or are now experiencing a bad year at the hands of an abusive administrator. I've had great, supportive administrators, but there came a time in my teaching career when I didn't think I was going to make it through the school year. It was a year that I want to forget, and I hope no teacher ever experiences a similar year, in which they are forced to stand up for unsound, unethical education practices that impede learning and prevent many students from achieving top academic performance, or are barred from performing at their optimum professional level. This is a story of the dark side of education. Now the Playbill for the story wouldn't have classified this as a comedy. However the events surrounding the story were comical—when I look at them in retrospect today. So it is okay to chuckle as you read this story. Here we have four characters; three administrators all who contrive to squash me because of one administrator's jealously, hatred, and anger against me. As a character I am an innocent teacher striving to fulfill the calling only to find myself in a battle with three mighty musketeers; only because they had more power than I. Being outwitted by me they began bickering among themselves, which gave me time to unloose the noose they had tightened around my neck. I rose to my feet, as if propelled by an explosive force and seized the opportunity to plan a response to this malicious treatment in a bedlam environment.

April 14, 2004, is a day I would not wish on any teacher. The day began as a productive one. The activity for the day was well planned; each class was fully engaged in the activity—working together, discussing a movie that followed the story of "The Jacket"—when suddenly, during fourth period, my building principal beckoned me and informed me that my supervisor had given me a poor evaluation. I felt as though my heart had stopped beating; I actually had trouble breathing. Finding composure so that I could get through the day was difficult. I was in a total daze the entire day. Before unfolding the events of this saga I'd like to briefly introduce the characters, whose names I would have taken pleasure to use, but I have not used their real names.

There is Mr. Elbert Rust who was the middle school principal, who often used awkward humor to bond with teachers; we shivered at the thought of him throwing an embarrassing comment at one of us. Many teachers knew he could not be trusted. Many of his staff questioned his ability and knowledge of how to operate a school, in light of the fact that he been an administrator for many years. The second player is Mrs. Sharon Clap, a new girl on the block from Arizona, whose short skirts often clung to her slim body. Mrs. Clap always walked with a springy bounce, and long purposeful strides. Even on relaxing days she walked as though there was something important she was about do. She was determined, confident, smart, but cunning and jealous and vengeful and would attack anyone who got in her way. Whereas, the last player Mr. Daniel Small, desperately wanted to be a school principal and was willing to "go along to get along with wrong to get to the top." He carried himself as a person who was already at the top: dressed the part, his salt and pepper hair was indication that he was a person of wisdom and well-versed on school policy and how to run a school. He was a down to earth person. There were many days when I would go into his office and he would share something funny, but clean. His warm smile was friendly, it was without malice and following that dreadful April

14, 2004, his smile turned apologetic. He carried himself with an air of authority. He was the smarter of the two administrators.

It happened like this. My administrator, a new vice-principal from Arizona, made it known that she was out to see me fail and had the audacity to let this be known to the department chair. The department chair shared the administrator's ploy. Shortly afterward, my career, personal life, health—mentally, physically, and spiritually—took a deep nosedive. My administrator made a conscious attempt to sabotage my credibility and ruin my professional career in education. For example, on a routine observation in October 2003, Mrs. Clap went through all of the paperwork on my desk. Shortly after, she requested a conference, and asked me to bring my attendance and grade book. Mrs. S.C. noticed that there were many unsatisfactory grades and reported that my lesson plans were not appropriate for my students. Excuse me, but if a student earns an "F" grade, that is the grade the student will get. Mrs. S.C. didn't agree with my logic. There was another occasion on which Mrs. S.C. observed me; although I was a post-probationary teacher, this was the third observation. What followed was another meeting. This time she wrote me up for not preparing an assessment that adequately represented student achievement. Mrs. S.C. did not ask for previous assessments, but based her observation on the midterm exam. Yes, a midterm exam. Sharon's unannounced visits continued; she made nine observations in all. She wrote me up for not having an academically focused learning environment, not wrapping up the learning activity appropriately, and not following the dean's behavior guidelines. This last referred to my sending a student to the dean's office for being tardy eighteen times. In the end, Mrs. Clap gave me a less than satisfactory performance evaluation, without following the district's guidelines for issuing such. The principal, Mr. Rust, rushed into my room, asked me to step outside for a moment, and whispered in my ear, "Mrs. Clap has just given you a poor evaluation." I guess you're feeling my heat. He went on to say, "I don't totally agree with her, but …" and left me standing in the hall in awe. I was abused by an administrator, actually both administrators. The saga doesn't end here.

I'm a fighter. I allowed myself twenty-four hours to grieve. I gathered my emotions and the fight was on. Mrs. Clap's unannounced classroom visits continued; this time, I documented every visit: when they occurred, what I was doing, what she did while in my room, and any messages she left with me. Each time, I followed up by requesting a teacher-administrator conference; she did not like this. At the conference I asked bold questions such as, "What was the nature of your visit? What did you find? What conclusions did you draw? What do I need to do to correct the problem—assuming there was one?"

I then typed out each conference and had it added to my file and requested that the district place a copy in her file. Let me tell you, she did not like that. Every single day, I vigilantly walked that campus and let her know I was not afraid of her; the battle was on and I intended to win. I demanded a district hearing; the right to such a hearing is a hidden policy all teachers should know about. At the hearing, the district officer commented, "Dr. Lindsey, your research, documentations, and requests are exemplary and commendable. You will hear from us very soon." The district's attorney and the hearing officer acknowledged that Mrs. Clap may have been harassing me. In the following year, 2005, the principal again assigned Mrs. Clap as my supervisor. You guessed it, she started out for me in August. Her harassment continued for two months, when I put my foot down and immediately contacted the regional superintendent; I was prepared to go public. Suddenly, I was assigned to another vice-principal. It didn't stop there. Mrs. Clap insisted that Mr. Small make unannounced visits; he made three and found nothing. Well, Mr. Small got fed up with Mrs. Clap's game and told her, "If you guys want to get that lady, you go ahead and get her, but look out because she's gonna fight back, and I can't see anything she is doing wrong as a teacher. In fact, she's going over and above the line of duty." The administrative harassment finally stopped. However, Mrs. Clap's career suffered. After interviewing for numerous principal positions, she failed and moved back to Arizona. Mr. Small was passed over numerous times for school district principal positions. As for the principal, Mr. Rust retired after the school district refused to allow him to open a new school. And so the story goes.

I healed, eventually, through God's grace and mercy, moved on, and started anew. What was meant for the bad turned out to be for the good. What worked for me was opening my life to healing. I turned to Philippians 3:13, which says: "One thing I do, forgetting what is behind and straining toward the goal to win the prize for which God has called heavenward in Christ Jesus." I also read Isaiah 43:18–19: "Forget the former things, do not dwell on the past. See, I am doing a new thing:

How it springs up; do you not perceive it? I am making a way in the desert and streams in the wasteland."

Grieving was definitely in order. Thus, that's what I did. I needed time to do that so that I could begin to heal. I stepped back and looked at how I needed to attack this problem. I made a plan of action; I kept my eyes and ears open, and kept detailed accounts of all visits (unannounced and announced) in a diary. I researched the school policy, carefully wrote my defense, and decided what my request was to be. I took action. This meant I needed to know the rules and the players. When it was over, I stood back, took a long breath, looked into the future, and realized that this too would pass.

Helen Keller said, "The marvelous richness of human experience would lose something of rewarding joy if there were not limitations to overcome. The hilltop hour would not be half so wonderful if there were no dark valleys to traverse."

The literature believes that retaining qualified teachers is a challenge for all districts across the country (Brownell et al., 1995). The literature states that "30 percent of beginning teachers exit the profession within their first two years" and "62 percent within five years." Brownell et al. (1995) go on to list three internal factors that affect teachers' decision to leave the profession: less than ideal working conditions, dissatisfaction with teacher salary, and the lack of administrative support. Let's talk briefly about the last factor: administrative support. A qualitative study on teacher attrition conducted by Gonzales and Brown (2008) reveals that the biggest reason teachers give for leaving the profession is administrative issues. The seven respondents cited numerous administrative issues teachers face for leaving the profession: Disrespect, put-downs, corrupt administrators, dishonesty and immoral conduct, lack of professional communication tactics, lack of support (administration takes side of student or parents), disregard for teacher assignment, and playing dirty politics. Teachers rely on the building administrator for information, feedback, and support. Teachers often complain that administrators don't keep them abreast of information that directly affects them and later hold them responsible for implementation. Teachers felt that they could not express opinions or had no voice. Many felt that administrators reprimanded them for speaking out; this leads to tension and creates a poor school environment. Harassment by administrators is the leading reason the nation experiences a tremendous loss of teachers to the teaching profession. A final example is a principal who instructed teachers to erase all zeros in their grade books and change failing grades, Fs and Ds, to Cs and then re-average the grades. If a teacher failed to follow administrator instructions, he or she could risk being written up for being insubordinate or face some other type of harassment. Here is where teachers need to know the district rules. Teachers need to assertively tell administrators how they wish to be treated. Far too many teachers allow administrators to treat them like furniture. This is one of the primary ways teachers lose the respect of parents and administrators. Lack of respect devalues the teaching profession. Teachers need to be willing to pay the cost of getting respect. It isn't students who take the joy out of teaching; it is administrators. Teachers give administrators and parents permission to treat them as less than human.

A personal note to teachers seriously considering teaching as a profession, those trying to stay in the profession, and those struggling to make that twenty-five- or thirty-year mark—need to gird up your loins. Get dressed in full armor to do battle with anyone or anything that entangles or strangles your desire to teach, so that you can take your stand against the enemy's schemes. Your struggle will be not against your students or parents, but against the rulers and authorities. Stand firm with the belt of integrity, breastplate of justice and courage, and shoes ready for any battle that comes your way.

Burned Out: Running on Empty

If a man does his best, what else is there?

— George S. Patton

Like most teachers, I was filled with enthusiasm, idealism, and hope about changing young minds. I was awed by the very magnitude of possibilities the education system offered. Well into my fifteenth year of teaching, I found myself still working seven days a week because I wanted to be the "exceptional teacher," the teacher who would turn around student apathy, improve swirling grades, and come up with a plan for keeping kids in school. I sacrificed my personal life for my work life; not a good exchange. Pretty soon, discontent set in: I did not have the principal's support, the student demographics changed and brought increased student apathy, the hours I spent at work increased. I constantly applied new instructional strategies to meet the demand of diverse cultures, and I used every opportunity to encourage student attendance. It became obvious that my students did not share my educational values. To them, school meant socializing, sports, fun, and not much else. So, when they did an assignment a "C" or "D" was okay. Their parents were grateful. Such attitudes lead to mediocre educational values. I began to feel exhausted because of the additional responsibilities placed on teachers: new instructional strategies every two weeks, more students; additional requirements to meet standards for No Child Left Behind; an ever-increasing class size. We were constantly developing pedagogical expertise alongside discipline and management skills—my class size still increased; new lesson plans were always being developed—my class size continued to swell, nothing done about that. The opportunities to move up the professional ladder became unavailable to me because of district politics. Things spiraled downward for the next few school years until I felt the wind of despair set in. I began to feel devalued. I often felt exhausted at the end of my workday; depression and sleepless nights set in. The school environment was less than positive for the students and teachers; not only was it increasingly difficult to motivate reluctant learners and encourage students who had attendance problems to come to school, but almost every day I would drive up to my workplace only to find that the school had been vandalized with graffiti the night before, the walls of the student bathroom had been written on or paper toweled, or the hall walls had holes in them. All of the emotional and mental trauma affected my work performance, even though I tried to leave my professional problems in the school parking lot.

Burnout is a psychological term for the experience of long-term exhaustion and diminished interest, while having too little time to recover (Kraft, 2006). This unhealthy condition can affect professionals in many disciplines, such as actors, musicians, mathematicians, authors, teachers, taxi drivers, athletes, and engineers. In the beginning, teaching seemed perfect; it was your way of "giving back," or "solving the world's ills through children," or believing teaching was fulfilling your "purpose" in life. So, you went into it with high hopes and expectations, and would rather teach than do anything else. This was my thinking. Little did I know that I was setting myself up for "occupational burnout," the most insidious and tragic kind of job stress. It often occurs when unrealistically high expectations and illusory and impossible goals are set (Miller and Smith, 2007). Miller and Smith assert that idealistic, hardworking perfectionists, self-motivated achievers with high aspirations and expectations, are on the road to burnout. Their unrealistic job expectations and goals lead to frustrations with themselves and the job itself, and failure often sets in. The burnout candidate's personality keeps him/her striving with intensity until he/she crashes, Miller and Smith have suggested that burnout falls into three stages:

- Honeymoon
During this period, years one through three, your job is like being

in heaven. You have lots of enthusiasm and motivation, and nothing seems impossible. You are pleased with your administrator, your colleagues, and your students and you can tolerate the curriculum and insurmountable responsibilities of being a teacher. You see no wrong.

- The Awakening

The awakening period runs from four to six years. The honeymoon period begins to wane and you awaken to the expectations, the staff, the administrator, the job of teaching. You now discover teaching isn't what you thought it would be, and you begin to question whether teaching is for you. You "discover" that teaching doesn't meet your needs, your administrator isn't as sound as you thought, your colleagues are mindless, and your students are apathetic about education. This leads to frustration. You begin to question your competence and ability.

- Burnout

It is at this point that you experience chronic fatigue and irritability, and frustration increases. Your eating and sleeping habits take a downward swirl. Typically, burnout can occur anytime after the first six years on the job. You become indecisive, your productivity drops, and you see less productivity in your students. You are likely to be absent from work a lot. You begin to look at avenues for escaping your burnout.

- Full-scale Burnout.

By this time, the professional is experiencing despair. This level can last indefinitely, perhaps as long as three to six years, as the professional doesn't realize what he or she is experiencing. The mental trauma is evident, but the professional doesn't assign a cause: there is depression, loss of confidence, loss of energy. The professional sees the profession as being less important, he or she is pessimistic, there is talk of quitting, and there is more complaining about the profession.

We all know that teaching is a challenging profession. A teacher's typical day begins early, often before 5:00 AM. The teacher quickly showers, brushes this and that, gobbles down his or her favorite cereal, and heads for the freeway. The teacher frantically fights through the 6:45 AM traffic, praying there is no accident along the way. There is a 7:15 AM parent conference this morning.

There are many days when there just isn't enough of a teacher to go around, enough time to cover all of a lesson, enough time to attend to every student, enough time to ensure that each student experiences a measure of success every day or enough time to implement the district's newest instructional strategy. I can't think of one teacher who doesn't have the students' best interests in mind. But the teacher must remember you can only do so much. To paraphrase words of wisdom from Mother Teresa, "In this life, we cannot do great things [all the time]. We can only do small things with great love [all the time]."

Teachers need to practice refueling, emotionally and physically, and to balance the demands of teaching. Challenge your burnout level by taking a simple quiz. Answer the following questions using a scale of one to four, with 1 being "never," 2 being "sometimes," 3 being "often," and 4 being "always":

- Do you take on more than your share of professional responsibilities?
- Do you do things in an effort to get approval from your administrator?
- Are you critical of how others do their jobs?
- Do you get angry or irritable with others?
- Do you raise your tone of voice when speaking with your students or staff members?
- Are you driven to get the job done?
- Do you seek to win or do better than others?
- Do you overlook the accomplishments of others?
- Do you take credit for doing something instead of giving credit to others?
- Do you like to take the lead?
- Are you impatient with other teachers who don't do things as you see fit, or who don't catch on to concepts as fast as you do?
- Do you find yourself driven to get things done according to your timetable?
- Do you feel that if you are not on one committee after another, things will not go well?
- Do you get involved in multiple school projects?
- Are you driven to meet deadlines?

- Do you take work home in lieu of relaxing and doing nothing?

Your answers may surprise you. The key below, with some small margin of error, will help identify your level of burnout.

If your score is:

16–26 it is likely that you are just going along, complacently on the job. This category indicates that you avoid burnout situations all together.

27–37 you have a balance in your ability to handle workplace situations; in other words you control your workplace situations.

38–48 your stress level is nearing burnout, you may be allowing stress to dictate your workplace situations. At this level, you should watch for signs of being extremely tense. Look back at the burnout signs I've mentioned, and identify stress areas that may be causing your burnout.

49–59 you are experiencing some forms of stress that are resulting in burnout. You might want to identify the stressful situations, and take measures to eliminate some or all of those situations.

60 you are in the danger zone, because you are burned out. I would seek medical attention.

Coping with burnout isn't always easy. It is one thing to ignore it and think it will go away, or shove it under a rug. That's a form of denial and not a healthy way of dealing with this psychological problem. Instead, recognize burnout for what it is: a form of illness that is curable. I chose to educate myself and get help. I became educated about what was happening in my life and took serious measures toward healing. I learned that burnout, if not treated, can lead to a stroke, suicide, or heart attack. I was determined not to leave the education profession in that state of mind. Adopting a lower-stress lifestyle, leaving your job at the end of your workday, and resting during vacations all lead to a more wholesome lifestyle. People who don't take time out look, feel, and behave as though life is out of balance.

Here are a few helpful suggestions for balancing the demands of teaching:

- Set realistic expectations and perspectives for yourself and your students.
- Reflect on your day, week, or month.
- Review your reason for being a teacher, administrator, or counselor.
- Use positive self-affirmations all day.
- Organize your living and work areas.
- Visualize positive outcomes. This may mean creating variety: doing old things in new ways.
- Take care of your health: keep physically fit, develop good eating habits.
- Meditate daily/count your blessings.
- Don't bring work home with you.
- Keep your life simple.
- Take time to laugh, play, and observe.
- Put forth your best; then stop.
- Learn to be patient.
- Take deep breaths and relax often.
- Say "No" more often.
- Focus on successes rather than on failures.
- Develop a forgiving attitude.
- Look at problems or setbacks as opportunities.
- Nurture your faith.

On your drive to work, listen to comforting music, or an audio tape. Keep a variety of tapes in your room for listening purposes: easy listening, jazz, opera, even Christian music.

Stop! Don't Eat That Doughnut

He who does not mind his belly will hardly mind anything else.

— *Samuel Johnson*

Nutrition is not my area of expertise, but I have spent a lot of time researching the relationship of nutrition to natural energy and to the psychology of stress. Both of these research areas affect an educator's performance. I've done research on eating properly. There was a time in my life, from the time I was a youngster right up to early adulthood, when I was overweight—okay, my doctor said I was "moderately obese." As a youngster, I didn't know what that word meant, until I got tired of being fat. Yep, I was so fat that climbing stairs was out of the question. When I got older and started to drive, I would park my car almost in the front door of any building; if I could have gotten a handicap sticker, I would have. But one day, I got tired of going through what fat people face each day: emotional and physical distress and embarrassment! Some fifteen years later, I still read nutritional articles, sides of boxes, and anything that speaks about healthy living, run fifteen miles a week, swim one hundred laps, and spin ride a bike for forty-five minutes. I can outrun the average high school kid. None of my degrees is in the medical area; the following suggestions are just that—suggestions— and they do not take the place of professional medical advice.

Your alarm goes off at 4:30 AM. You quickly hit the snooze button and pull the covers over your head. "Just five more minutes," you beg. Thoughts of writing lesson plans, writing referrals, sitting in on a parent conference, making parent phone calls, and a staff meeting plague you.

You crawl out of bed and moan to yourself, "I can't face this day; I need to call in sick." You figure a shower and a couple of cups of strong black coffee will do it. You manage to get yourself dressed, the kids off to school, and you and your spouse out the door. Just about mid-morning, 10:00 AM, sitting at your computer taking attendance, you begin to nod off and you catch your fingers drifting down the keyboard. So you quickly eat the doughnut you grabbed from the teachers' lounge. It's actually your second doughnut. At noon, just two hours after the doughnut, you're feeling low, sort of depressed, and yucky. You head for the soda machine and get a coke to eat, along with a cafeteria dish: mashed potatoes drenched in gravy, peas straight out of the can, and fried, breaded chicken fingers.

When your workday ends, you are really feeling brain-dead. You hope you don't fall asleep at the wheel, because you still have to pick up the kids and stop by the store.

If this sounds like you, you are suffering from a gradual decline in your ability to produce energy. It shows up in how we look, think, feel, work, and play; it also affects the aging process. You may argue that "it's old age" or "I'm not as young as I used to be." But energy decline happens to young people, too. When your cells are producing energy easily, you have more stamina to get through the day. You actually feel great. We all need energy to accomplish our daily goals and meet the demands essential for life. However, as we get older our bodies change, and our energy-producing systems change, too.

We can't eat those fat-saturated delicious meals or snacks like we used to. Our metabolisms slow down considerably; sometimes our thinking isn't as sharp or we become less creative. We move more slowly, our muscles are weakened, and our hearts may not beat as efficiently. Recent research pinpointed in JAMA (2009) indicates that a healthy lifestyle pays off in prevention of cardiovascular disease. The report goes on to say that men who exercised on a regular basis, drank moderately, were not smokers, who weren't overweight, and who included cereals, fruit, fresh vegetables showed a lower risk of heart failure. These findings are important as heart failure is the primary cause of acute hospital visits. It also is the most prevalent chronic cardiovascular ailment (JAMA, 2009). Alongside the cardiovascular issue is a study involving more than 55,000 women and hypertension

(JAMA, 2009). This study found that women who adhere to a modified lifestyle have a lower incidence of hypertension.

Healthy eating habits result in a healthy diet that is balanced, free of high-calorie foods, and varied. You might consider eating foods rich in nutrients, such as fruits, vegetables, and whole grains; don't forget the fish, especially salmon. That means you'll need to get rid of unhealthy eating habits or eating unhealthy foods like candy, soda, French fries, and potato chips, anything that includes of trans saturated fats or monounsaturated fats. A healthy diet is low in cholesterol and sodium and limits the intake of foods high in the glycemic index. The glycemic index measures the effect a high-carbohydrate food has on one's blood sugars; some researchers contend that foods lower in the glycemic index causes smaller increases in blood sugar, and are better for your health (Mayo, 2009). Here are some simple suggestions for recharging your energy level and helping you eat a healthier diet.

Get rid of the sugar. We are often told to eat something with sugar to raise our energy level. The energy boost we get from eating that candy bar, soda, white rice, white bread, pastas made from white flours, or doughnuts is short-lived. Why? Because it gives you a quick high, but shortly afterward, you will feel down, maybe even depressed or tired. According to an article in *Nutrition Action Health Letter* (2004), doughnuts have a double dose of fats, trans and saturated. You might want to try these foods instead: alfalfa sprouts in a spinach salad; one medium red or green apple; or coconut, pineapple, or apricots. Try broccoli, brown rice, or other whole grains; beans, lentils, and other legumes; yogurt; or low-fat popcorn. For example, a high-energy lunch would be a spinach salad with cheese or tofu or grilled chicken, and a tuna salad sandwich on brown bread. Half of a baked potato, no butter or sour cream, with a bit of low-fat, low-carb cheese, is great. Check with your doctor about salt, salty foods, and coffee. I don't use salt, nor do I drink coffee. Water is the best drink ever. Or you can drink vegetable, orange, or apple juice in modest portions.

Try to include more fish and poultry and less other types of meat. Avoid fried foods, simply because they are high in fat content from the oil they are prepared in; baked French fries are actually good. Stay away from salt. Your food is naturally salty, and when you add salt the sodium increases your body fluids; that, in turn, increases your blood pressure, and the resulting hypertension can lead to heart disease or stroke. A high-salt diet is more than 1.5 per 100g (*Wellsphere*, 2009) Don't eat more than four eggs a week, as they are high in cholesterol. If you like eggs, try egg whites. They taste great and are better for you. And, for those terrible, horrible, no-good, very bad days when all you want is a refreshing glass of wine or a beer, do enjoy with moderation. Most alcoholic drinks are high in calories.

I know that by the early afternoon, we generally get tired or hungry. How about a snack? I look forward to my snacks. I usually munch on almonds, walnuts, dried fruit, or even a granola bar. If you eat nutritionally, you probably won't need supplements (and consult your physician before taking any supplements). Eating right will give you more energy, and you'll be ready to take on whatever the day brings

A Teacher's Hands

It is noble to teach oneself, but still nobler to teacher others—and less trouble.

— *Mark Twain*

The end of each school year sees many teachers exit the teaching profession. Many have braved the classroom for fifteen, twenty, thirty, even thirty-five years. I recall a colleague saying, "Teaching has changed in the last fifteen of my thirty-two years. There were times when I could hardly face another day." My friend, Mrs. Rhodes, recounted her teaching experiences with pleasure, as joy bubbled in her laughter and shone in her eyes. I shall forever remember the cheer she wore on her face as she greeted each student, making them all feel special.

As a kindergarten teacher, she held the hands of many kindergarten children. Her calming words comforted their crying eyes. To get their attention she would often sing in a gently soft tone, "Are you listening? Are you listening, little ones?" They would be sitting up straight, with smiling faces and folded arms just waiting for the next verse. It was an amazing sight to see. Her warm hug eased their tender little hurts. Her tenderness didn't stop with the kindergarteners, but when she became a second grade teacher she maintained the same exuberance.

As a second grade teacher, she was astonished at the sense of fulfillment she felt as my friend taught her students how to behave responsibly, how to be kind when they play, and how to be fair. She gave each student her love and allowed them to be creative. During math time, should a student forget what two plus two equaled, she would help the child remember, and say, "I know you have the answer." She gave her students hope and made them feel valued.

With arthritic hands, she showed her students how to make Japanese carp kites, with colored tissue paper. The students decorated their kites and went out on the playground to fly them.

My friend never forgot her students when she traveled during the summer. Her stories of travel, pictures, and artifacts were meant to encourage her students to travel, in order to expand their minds and their world. My friend made reading time come alive. She recalls using puppets to tell a short story. Her students' eyes were glued to the dancing puppets. She knew the importance of knowing how to read; yet, she also knew how difficult it was to get students to read. She believed that teachers should be able to take any subject area and make the subject fun and the learning experience successful.

Throughout her years as a teacher, my friend's hands touched many students; she cheered when her students won the second grade spelling bee contest; she clapped when one of her students was chosen as citizen of the month; and she always made certain each student's birthday was a big celebration in her class. Even though she has left the classroom, her inspiration continues with colleagues and former students.

As my friend exited the teaching profession she continued to use her hands to wish others well; to point someone else down the right road; to cheer another soul, and to celebrate her life. Her hands rocked the cradle and ruled in the hearts of thousands of other people's children.

Final Words

No other profession is like teaching. Teachers touch our world in so many ways. Teachers touch lives. Teachers mold and shape lives. Teachers build bridges that prepare students to cross from one stage of their lives into another. Teachers remain the most influential people in the world.

Les Brown, a motivational speaker, shared a story in *Live Your Dreams*, about how Mr. Washington, one of his eleventh-grade teachers, touched his life. He was in high school, but that teacher's influence remains a fresh memory today. There are so many teachers whose influence parallels that of Mr. Washington. I realize that school districts across the country have taken strong measures to raise student achievement, improve standards for student learning, and develop improved standards for how student achievement is measured. As a result of No Child Left Behind, schools that have not shown academic improvement have been sanctioned. Our educational institutions continue to encounter huge challenges in improving student achievement, hiring and retaining indispensable teachers, improving the quality of instruction, creating and maintaining classroom management, and developing stronger discipline procedures in our schools.

Research indicates that when teachers have a thorough knowledge of pedagogy, the level of instruction improves (Rivkin, Hanushek, and Kain, 1998). As stories in this book have documented many times, there are practices teacher still need to demonstrate and new teachers need to improve: developing engaging lessons for reluctant learners, understanding and designing instruction that entices the unmotivated learner, planning instruction and designing enrichment activities for all students, developing comprehensive assessments beyond the objective-type measuring tools, developing creative ways to get parents involved in the education process, applying the principles for writing useful, creative lesson plans, and continuing to become professionally responsible.

This book identifies areas of teacher education that many educational programs leave out, school districts and educational programs need to evaluate their teacher-education programs to ensure that they provide new teachers with a toolkit filled with rich teaching craft that they can utilize with diverse learners; this means working with school leaders' operational goals.

Teaching and teachers should be approached from a positive framework. If we encore the assumption and old adage that "all students are capable of learning," then we must also believe that "all teachers can teach, given the right environment, support, and opportunities to implement differentiated instruction." When these basic needs are in place, there will be improved teaching and successful student academic performance.

Bibliography

Alliance for Excellent Education (2005). " Teacher Attrition: A Costly Loss to the Nation and States," *Issue Brief.* Washington DC: Alliance for Excellent Education.

Bandura, A. (1997). *Self-Efficacy: The Exercise of Control.* New York: Freeman.

Biscay, Andre (Fall 1996). "Teacher Motivation and Job Satisfaction: A Study Employing the Experience Sampling Method. *Journal of Psychology* 3: 147–154.

Bomia, L., Beluzo, L., Demeester, D., Elander, K., Johnson, M., Sheldon, B. (1997). *The Impact of Teaching Strategies on Intrinsic Motivation.* Champaign, IL.: ERIC clearing House on Elementary and Early Childhood Education.

Brophy, Jere E. 1998. *Motivating Students to Learn.* Boston: McGraw Hill.

Brownell, M., Smth, S., McNellis, J. and Lenk, L. (1995). "Career Decisions in Special Education: Current and Former Teachers' Personal Views." *Exceptionality* 5. 83–102.

Burns, D. (2008). "Differentiation for Reluctant Learners," ASCD conference, June, 2008, on Differentiated Instruction, Understanding by Design, and What Works in Schools, Nashville, TN.

Charles, C., (2005), *Building Classroom Discipline*. New York: Pearson.

Collins, Marva (1992*)*. *Ordinary Children, Extraordinary Teachers*. Charlottesville, VA: Hampton Roads Publishing.

Duke, Daniel, ed. (1979). Classroom Management. *Yearbook of the National Society for the Study of Education*. Chicago: University of Chicago Press.

Evertson, C.M., Emmer, E.T., & Worsham, M.E. (2003). *Classroom Management For Elementary Teachers* (6th ed.). Boston: Allyn Bacon.

Gonzales, L. and Brown, M.S. (Mar. 2008). "Teachers Who Left the Teaching Profession: A Qualitative Understanding." *The Qualitative Report* (13)1. 1–11.

Griffith, D. (2009). *Disruptive Behavior: Tips for Classroom Management*. San Jose, CA: San JoseState UP.

Hayashi, Leslee A. (2002). *Fables from the Sea* (2002). Honolulu: Mutual Publishing of Hawaii.

Hicks, C. Glasgow and McNary, S. (2004). What Successful Mentors Do: Research-based Strategies for New Teachers' Induction, Training and Support. Thousand Oaks, CA: Corwin Press.

Hurley, J., Liebman, B (Jan.–Feb. 2004). "The Hole Truth: What You Don't Know about Doughnuts—Brand-name Rating." Health Publications.

Ingersoll, R.M. (2002). "The Teacher Shortage: A Case of Wrong Diagnosis and Wrong Prescription." *NASSP Bulletin,* 86, 16–31.

Ingersoll, R.M. (2006). "The Teacher Shortage: A Case of Wrong Diagnosis and Wrong Prescription." Presentation acquired via personal communication, May 2006.

Kraft, U. (June/July 2006). "Burned Out." *Scientific American Mind*. 29–33.

Krause, Robert (1994). *Fables Aesop Never Wrote*. Toronto, Canada: Penguin Group.

Marshall, Marvin (2005). *Discipline Without Stress, Punishments or Rewards*. Los Alamitos, CA: Piper Press.

Marzano, R.J. with Marzano, J.S. and Pickering, D.J. (2003b). "Classroom Management that Works." Alexandria, VA: ASCD.

Marzano, R.J. (2003). "What Works in Schools." Alexandria, VA: ASCD.

Mayo Foundation. *Healthy Diet: End the Guesswork with these Nutrition Guidelines.* Nutrition Action Healthletter, Foundation for Medical Education and Research, Feb. 13, 2009.

McCombs, B.C. and Pope, J. E. (1994). *Motivating Hard to Reach Students.* Washington DC: American Psychological Association.

McGrew, K. and Evans, J. (2009). "Expectations for Students with Cognitive Disabilities: Is the Cup Half Empty or Half Full? Can the Cup Flow Over?" *Synthesis Report 55*, Minneapolis: National Center on Educational Outcomes, Univ. of Minnesota.

McKinney, K. (2009). *Encouraging Students' Intrinsic Motivation.* Normal, IL: Illinois State UP.

Mendler, A., and Curwin, R. (1999). *Discipline with Dignity for Challenging Youth.* Bloomington, IN: National Education Service.

Miller, Lyle and Smith, Alma Dell (2007). "Anxiety at Work—the Road to Burnout." *Healthyplace: America's Mental Health Channel.* www.healthyplace.com/anxiety-panic/main/anxiety-at-work-the-road-to-burnout/menu-id-69/. Accessed Feb. 19, 2007.

Moore, Johnson, S. (2006). "Why New Teachers Stay," American Federation of Teachers, Summer 2006. The Project on the Next Generation of Teachers, Washington DC.

New-Nouveau Brunswick Department of Education, Student Services, (2000). "Effective Instructional Methods." New Brunswick, Canada.

Price, William and Terry, Ernest (July 29, 2008). "Can Small Class Sizes Help Retain Teachers to the Profession?" Houston, TX: National Council of Professors of Educational Administrators,

Remen, Naomi (2000). *My Grandfather's Blessings.* New York: Penguin Putnam.

Rivkin, S., Hanushek, E. and Kain,J. (2000). "Teachers, Schools and Academic Achievement": J. NBER Working Paper—W6691 (National Bureau of Economic Research). June 1998, revised 2000, Washington DC.

Schunk, D. H., Pintrich, A. (2001). *Motivation in Education: Theory, Research and Applications.* Englewood Cliffs, NJ: Prentice Hall.

Smith, T. and Ingersoll, R. (2004). "Reducing Teacher Turnover: What Are the Components of Effective Induction?" *American Educational Research Journal,* 41(2), 681–714.

Smith, T. and Ingersoll, R. (2003). "The Wrong Solution to the Teacher Shortage." *Educational Leadership,* 60(8), 30–3.

Stenlund, K. (1995). "Teacher Perceptions Across Cultures: The Impact of Students on Teacher Enthusiasm and Discouragement in a Cross-cultural Context." *Journal of Education Research* (41) 2, 145–61.

Strong, R., Silver, H., Robin, A. (1995). "What Do Students Want?" *Educational Leadership* 53 (1) 8–12.

Sullo, B. (2007). *Activating the Desire to Learn.* Alexandria, VA: Association for Supervision and Curriculum Development.

Wellsphere (Mar. 19, 2009). How Much Salt is Good for Me?

West, Ross (1990). How to be happy in the job you sometimes can't stand. Broadman Press, Nashville, Tenn.

Wolk, Barbara (Mar. 25, 2008). "How Do You Motivate the Reluctant Learner?" ASCD Inservice, Alexandria, VA.

Lumsden, L. Teacher Morale, "ERIC" Clearinghouse in Educational Management, 120, (March, 1998). ED 422601.

Penedergast, D. & Bahr, N. (2006). Taking Middle Years Rethinking Curriculum, Pedagogy and Assessment. Crows Nest, N. S.W.: Allen & Unwin, 2005, 211.

Pianta, R. Enhancing Relationships Between Children and Teachers. Washington, D.C.: American Psychological Assn., 1999.

Motshinig-Pitrik, "R. Figl, K. Cornelius-White, Hoey A. (2004). Person-Centered Education: A Meta-Analysis of Care in Progress. Journal of Border Educational Research, 3 (1), 81-87.

Stipek, D. Relationships Matter. Educational Leadership. Sept. 2006, 64 (1), p. 46-49.

Djoussee, L., Driver JA, Gazioano JM., Relation between modifiable lifestyle factors and lifetime risk of heart failure. JAMA, 2009l 302: 394-400.

Roger V. Lifestyle and cardiovascular health: JAMA, 2009: 302: 437-439.

Forman, JP. Stampfer, MJ., Curhan, GC., Diet and lifestyle risk factors associated with incident hypertension in women. JAMA, 2009, 302: 402-411.